THE ULTIMATE COMPLEX PTSD TREATMENT GUIDE

FROM TRAUMA, FEAR, ANXIETY, PANIC ATTACKS, DEPRESSION, AND STRESS TO SAFETY, INTERNAL WELL-BEING, AND INNER FULFILLMENT

ANDREI NEDELCU

© COPYRIGHT 2023 - ALL RIGHTS RESERVED.

The content contained within this book may not be reproduced, duplicated, or transmitted without direct written permission from the author or the publisher.

Under no circumstances will any blame or legal responsibility be held against the publisher, or author, for any damages, reparation, or monetary loss due to the information contained within this book, either directly or indirectly.

Legal Notice:

This book is copyright protected. It is only for personal use. You cannot amend, distribute, sell, use, quote, or paraphrase any part, or the content within this book, without the consent of the author or publisher.

Disclaimer Notice:

Please note the information contained within this document is for educational and entertainment purposes only. All effort has been executed to present accurate, up-to-date, reliable, and complete information. No warranties of any kind are declared or implied. Readers acknowledge that the author is not engaged in the rendering of legal, financial, medical, or professional advice. The content within this book has been derived from various sources. Please consult a licensed professional before attempting any techniques outlined in this book.

By reading this document, the reader agrees that under no circumstances is the author responsible for any losses, direct or indirect, that are incurred as a result of the use of the information contained within this document, including, but not limited to, errors, omissions, or inaccuracies.

CONTENTS

Introduction   *7*

1 All You Need to Know About CPTSD   11
2 Exploring the Consequences of CPTSD   24
3 Reordering Your Neural Network and Pathways   38
4 Recovering From CPTSD by Understanding Trauma   50
5 Healing CPTSD by Working on Your Body   62
6 Healing CPTSD Through Emotional Support   78
7 Healing CPTSD by Making Different Choices   91
8 Healing CPTSD Using Exposure Therapy   107
9 Healing CPTSD by Communicating Your Inner World   119
10 Healing CPTSD by Dealing With Negative Emotions   131
11 Healing CPTSD by Creating Safe Spaces   143
12 How to Live Peacefully and Happily With CPTSD   155

Conclusion   *165*
References   *169*

INTRODUCTION

The first childhood memories that still stick with me are images of my dad beating up my mom. Our family kept that secret for years. It became something separating me and my younger brother from our classmates. We didn't make friends, for friends always wanted to visit our home, have sleepovers and playdates, and we could never take that risk. Our secret was hiding behind closed doors in our home, and we couldn't allow any strangers onto this territory. It would blow the cover we thought we had.

It has been about 10 years since I've been old enough to escape this secret. As I finished school, I got a job, saved some money, and got an apartment on the other side of the city. Nothing fancy, just a tiny place where there were no secrets. I asked my brother to join me in this safe haven, but he didn't want to leave my mother's side. I invited my mother, and she didn't want to leave her husband.

Five years later, my dad hit my mom for the last time. She fell and hit her head. After two weeks in a coma, she passed away. My brother took care of my dad before he vanished overnight. I've heard he is hanging out in the dark alleys at night, seeking the shadows to hide from the police. I lost my mother. I lost my brother. I lost my childhood. I never went back to that place. Yet, I still haven't been able to escape the prison in my head. It's keeping me there even though I am not.

Complex Post Traumatic Stress Disorder, or CPTSD, is caused by prolonged exposure to trauma. It is a severe mental health concern that impacts every aspect of your life. While it wraps you in a blanket of isolation, the relationships you manage to maintain are often rocky, for you're mostly irritable. Then there is the immense guilt always overshadowing your life.

Reliving these moments consumes your thoughts, mostly at night, keeping sleep at bay. While this insomnia harms your physical health, your mental and emotional health is shattered too. Suicide rates are more than four times higher among those with CPTSD (Lane, 2020). You're alive, but you're simply just not living.

Yet, this is a prison you can choose to break free from. The doors can open wide and you can be free by making minor changes to your life, perspective, behavior, and choices. Yes, just like many other patients seeing me as their mental health care provider, you, too, can step out of the shadows and into the light of happiness.

In this book, I share the same guidance and advice that I share with those who I help in my practice. The questions in every chapter will direct you toward similar introspection. The outcome you can expect is the same as for them. Yes, I promise you ultimate freedom, satisfaction, joy, fulfillment, and hope for the future.

We'll explore the nature of CPTSD and what sets it apart from PTSD. While getting familiar with the nature of your mental state, and any severe mental health concerns, is a great foundation to start this journey, it isn't enough. No, we'll also explore the many resources you have access to that you likely haven't been able to identify. We'll ponder the steps you can take to care for your mind and body and how to establish and use social support networks to aid you on this journey. Exploring useful aids will be an incomplete venture without considering formal treatment options, so we'll touch on these too.

I've seen what mental entrapment looks like and the severe adversities patients face when they seek my help. But I've also witnessed recovery and what it means to break free from a prison you thought you'd never be freed from, and I promise you that this is the kind of freedom available to you too.

A stern warning, though—the longer you wait to seek help, the worse your concern will become. Often, this happens for no other reason than the sheer exhaustion of being trapped that causes you to lose hope. Once helplessness steps in, it becomes so much harder to take the steps toward taking control of your life.

So, don't delay any longer. Reclaim your life. You might not have had any control over your circumstances and what happened to you. You might have been disempowered, vulnerable, and incapable of preventing the trauma you've been exposed to, but now it is different. Now you can choose freedom. Now you can take steps to get back into your life and live it as fully as managing CPTSD is possible.

Make that choice today!

1

ALL YOU NEED TO KNOW ABOUT CPTSD

When all you know is fight or flight, red flags and butterflies all feel the same. –Cindy Cherie

The impact of trauma can last for only a short while, but in these few short minutes, or even seconds, it can change your entire world and years can go by before you find your footing in life again.

MIKE'S STORY

Before throwing back his duvet, the alarm catches Mike's eye. The large fluorescent numbers remind him how long sleep has been evading him. It would help if he could close his eyes, but often when he does, he is instantly met with the bright lights in his eyes, the screeching of tires, screams, cracking glass, and the blood-chilling noise of the car's body crushed by the stone and rock as it rolled down the cliff. It has been three years since the accident, but still, he can't get the image out of his mind. Nor can he shed the smell of dust and fuel lingering in the air. Then, there is crying, the little girl trapped in the vehicle, the only voice in the quiet night. One shrill scream before the explosion silences it.

He needs air. His body is tired and severely sleep-deprived, but he walks out into the night, down the street, until he finds himself on a bench at the quay, several miles from his home. Just before the break of dawn, four youngsters approached him.

From the moment he saw the shadows heading his way, he knew they were trouble. "Where is your car, man?" the first one shouted at him. "Dude, just give us your keys. We won't hurt you. We need a ride."

They didn't believe him, that he walked there, that he didn't own a car. Or that he will never get behind the steering wheel ever again. They called him a freak before beating him up.

The sun was high when a fisherman found him. "Can I call someone to help you?" the man asked.

"No," Mike answered.

"No?" the man asked, confused.

"No one. No one can help me," Mike said before getting up to stumble back home.

These images, the horror that appears real during his dreams, are merely figments of what happened, now trapped in his head. But the reality of Mike's life is that he is all alone. Since the accident, Mike has distanced himself from everyone in his life. There is nobody who can help him.

Nightmares, insomnia, flashbacks, and distancing from others are only some of the many symptoms of PTSD controlling Mike's life. But what exactly is PTSD? Are you familiar with the term? An even more critical question is do you experience similar symptoms as Mike?

WHAT IS POST-TRAUMATIC STRESS DISORDER?

It is still far too often the case that post-traumatic stress disorder (PTSD) is considered a mental health concern only linked to veterans or others who have faced combat or served in emergency services. This misunderstanding of mental health conditions is likely due to it often being referred to as shell shock, battle fatigue, or combat disorder. While it is usually diagnosed in those instances, it would be a mistake to assume it is only linked to those who served in any of these capacities.

When someone is an eyewitness or victim of a traumatic event this exposure can lead to PTSD. During this exposure, the person perceives the traumatic event as physically and/or emotionally threatening. This exposure can impact their mental, social, physical, and spiritual well-being. Combat is an example of such an event, but it can also be caused by events like the accident Mike continues to relive. Other causes are rape or sexual assault, natural disasters, bullying, historical trauma, terrorist attacks, or a violent intimate partner. I must emphasize that PTSD is a severe psychiatric disorder that can occur after any traumatic event.

The symptoms of PTSD manifest in several ways and are immensely disruptive to everyday life. Symptoms included dealing with unwanted memories triggered by unexpected stimuli. These memories of the traumatic event are upsetting and can leave those with PTSD severely distraught. These memories can also surface at night, resulting in constant nightmares and insomnia, and the lack of sleep can impact overall wellness.

Needless to say, much effort goes into avoiding exposure to emotional triggers. It means the person avoids talking about the event or visiting places that resemble the place where the trauma occurred.

On an emotional level, symptoms include feeling detached, struggling to sustain healthy relationships, emotional numbness, lack of interest in activities that the person enjoyed in the past, and harboring a negative perspective on the world and people in it.

Behavioral changes include constant awareness, reacting with fear, being vigilant all the time, and being easily startled or frightened. This is a high-stress state to be in, which will, over time, have an immensely negative impact on your physical health.

Before I expand on the differences between complex post-traumatic disorder and PTSD, I want to highlight that PTSD is usually linked to once-off exposure to trauma, compared to CPTSD, which is associated with exposure to multiple or a series of traumatic events.

WHAT IS NOT CPTSD?

When was the first time you heard the term CPTSD? Don't worry if this is the first time, for in comparison with PTSD, CPTSD is far less known. This is not because it is a less common mental health concern but because it is often confused with other mental health challenges, like Borderline Personality Disorder (BPD).

BORDERLINE PERSONALITY DISORDER

The symptoms of CPTSD and BPD are so similar that confusing the two mental health concerns is easy. CPTSD may be mistaken for BPD because it is the lesser known of the two. However, there are some key differences to be aware of:

- The symptoms of BPD fluctuate—at times, it is present, and at other times it is not, while CPTSD symptoms remain present.

- CPTSD is often linked to feelings of shame, guilt, and fear, while BPD centers around boredom and emptiness.

- BPD is associated with reckless behavior, while CPTSD is linked to avoidance behavior.

- In BPD, you'll witness episodes of dissociative behavior, while CPTSD is linked to emotional flashbacks that can be highly upsetting.

The origin of BPD is rooted in a combination of genetic and environmental factors, while CPTDS is caused by long-term exposure to trauma. We are specifically considering events like domestic abuse or assault, either in the past or ongoing. Then there is also maltreatment or abandonment during the early years, or witnessing any domestic violence or abuse over an extended time that can contribute to CPTSD.

ENDURING PERSONALITY CHANGES AFTER CATASTROPHIC EVENTS

Another mental health concern similar to CPTSD is enduring personality changes after catastrophic events (EPCACE). Remember that exposure to natural disasters, warfare, or terrorist attacks can lead to CPTSD, and these are all also causes that can result in EPCACE. While the origins of the two mental health concerns are similar, they are not the same, and misdiagnosing CPTSD as EPCACE can hinder effective treatment. A diagnosis of EPCACE requires a patient to show the symptoms for at least two years after the trauma. This requirement means that the patient has to show long-term symptoms before effective treatment can be applied. However, today the World Health Organization (WHO) doesn't recognize EPCACE as a condition anymore as it gives preference to a diagnosis of PTSD. That said, some mental health experts still use EPCACE.

DISORDERS OF EXTREME STRESS NOT OTHERWISE SPECIFIED

Then we also need to notice disorders of extreme stress not otherwise specified (DESNOS). DESNOS has similar symptoms and causes to CPTSD and is therefore often used as a replacement term, especially by mental health professionals in the United States.

WHAT DOES IT MEAN TO LIVE WITH CPTSD?

In the next chapter, we'll delve into the details of the symptoms of CPTSD, but for now, it is important to highlight that life with CPTSD can be challenging, even more so if it isn't diagnosed or misdiagnosed.

It is a condition linked to feelings of utter worthlessness. This low self-esteem robs you of the confidence to take control of your life. It can even rob you of the confidence to take action to manage your condition, as it may seem that whatever is wrong with you is just so much stronger than you so even trying to manage it is an impossible quest. This lack of self-esteem also often manifests as persistent self-blame. Regardless of what happens, you can get stuck in a downward spiral of believing everything is your fault. This is, of course, a highly disempowering approach to life.

Emotional dysfunction is one of the critical distinguishing symptoms of CPTSD. The term emotional dysfunction refers to experiencing intense emotions. For example, it is normal to feel sad or angry sometimes, but when dealing with CPTSD, these feelings are much more severe. While a healthy experience will only take you off course for a short while or have a limited impact on your life, these emotions can be overwhelming and last much longer. It is also common for patients with CPTSD to describe themselves as living within a dream and like none of their experiences are real. Happiness seems to evade them constantly, and finding joy or satisfaction in their lives can be tough.

As the origins of CPTSD are primarily rooted in some abusive relationship or having a relationship with the abuser whose abuse they've often witnessed, it is hard for the person suffering from CPTSD to develop a healthy relationship with anyone. Even their relationship with the abuse is unhealthy and can be challenging to end. While they are often aware that what they experience in the relationship is bad for them, the person who is being abused often decides to stay simply because of familiarity with this bond. It is a highly complex set of feelings that may be harbored toward the abuser, and breaking this bond isn't easy.

CPTSD VS. PTSD

While CPTSD is in many ways like PTSD, some features set these two disorders apart. The first significant difference between the two psychological disorders is that PTSD is linked to a single traumatic event, compared to CPTSD resulting from long-term exposure to trauma.

As a result of this difference, we can't deny that those dealing with CPTSD were also exposed to feeling trapped in their situation. It is not only the trauma they experienced that is a significant concern, but also the sense of helplessness they developed as an escape from their situation was impossible. It could be that they were captured, and escaping wasn't possible. In this case, survivors of human trafficking come to mind. It can be that escaping was too dangerous and that fear for their lives kept them trapped in repeated traumatic exposure. This is a position many refugees and those trapped in warfare find themselves in. Or, perhaps, they had to stay because they depended on the person who was keeping them trapped for their survival. For example, a child exposed to sexual abuse may have no means to run away and therefore has to stay in such a dreaded situation. The perpetrator could've had an emotional influence over them. For example, a mother suffering physical spousal abuse who can't leave as that would mean she has to leave her kids behind. So, it is essential to remember that PTSD results from episodic exposure, while CPTSD is linked to chronic exposure.

As CPTSD develops due to prolonged exposure, the symptoms resulting from this kind of exposure also vary from PTSD to a certain extent. Some symptoms associated with CPTSD are emotional dysregulation and challenges with interpersonal relationships, or even a fear of such relationships. It is common to see excessive emotional reactions from victims of these types of trauma. They experience difficulty concentrating and will often drift off mid-conversation. Their self-perception is immensely skewed. It is quite common that they have such a negative self-perception that they may even be convinced they deserve to be exposed to the trauma. This is met with a similarly skewed perception of the perpetrator, who is often considered powerful or almighty and deserving of pleasure derived from their behavior toward the victim.

When we compare these symptoms to the classic fear-based symptoms of PTSD and how it instills excessive anxiety in the person with PTSD, it is evident that there are vast differences despite the similarities. In PTSD cases, it is more common to see someone experience hypervigilance, being on edge, and exaggerated responses. At the same time, a lot of avoidance occurs to avoid triggers causing flashbacks to the traumatic event.

PTSD and CPTSD may appear very similar, but they're not. The causes of your condition vary, and so, even to a minimal extent, do your symptoms. Have you been diagnosed with PTSD but aren't convinced that is the battle you're facing? Are the treatment options you've been relying on not bringing you the outcome you've hoped for? Then, maybe it is time to get a second opinion to ensure you're correctly diagnosed.

- What are the symptoms you're experiencing?
- What are the events in your past causing your mental health challenges?
- What are the triggers you're aware of?
- What are the main concerns keeping you from sleeping or chasing you in your dreams?

QUICK RECAP

Mental health problems don't define who you are. They are something you experience. You walk in the rain and you feel the rain, but you are not the rain. –Matt Haig

While there are many corresponding symptoms between CPTSD and PTSD and other mental health concerns, it is vital to get an accurate diagnosis. Once your mental health challenge has been accurately identified, you can take the necessary steps to get familiar with it and better manage it effectively.

So, don't fear a positive diagnosis of CPTSD as this is the first step towards taking the necessary action, getting yourself in a position to begin to manage your mental health concern and its symptoms effectively. It is a way to regain quality of life and live freely, experiencing joy and lasting healthy relationships.

2

EXPLORING THE CONSEQUENCES OF CPTSD

Except for having a greater understanding of how CPTSD impacts the brain structure and processes, we also need to explore how it affects the lives of those dealing with CPTSD. One of these challenges is difficulty in maintaining personal relationships as we can see in the story of Mila and Steve

MILA AND STEVE

Mila and Steve met at a fundraiser for a charity offering support to refugees. Steve was one of the caterers at the event. Mila was one of the speakers who shared her story of escape and the challenges she and her family faced when they became refugees. Their romance bloomed from the moment they bumped into each other by accident.

Initially, nothing kept the two apart, but over recent months, Steve isn't sure whether Mila is the right person to spend his life with. Everything was so great for the first couple of months, but then she became distant like she was avoiding him. For days, he wouldn't hear anything from her. She wouldn't answer his calls, reply to his texts, or call him back. She was cold towards him when they saw each other, almost like she wasn't present. When he asked her about it, she would brush it off at first but later became defensive, screaming at him that he wanted to control her life. There have been a couple of times when he was sure he needed to end the relationship, but then she would become kind again like she was when he met her.

"I don't know, man. It is all so confusing. I thought I met the woman I wanted to spend the rest of my life with when I met her. She was just so amazing. You know, I knew she had a difficult past, but she always came across so strong, like she just stood tall like a tree in the wind when others tumbled from a slight breeze. But now? Geez, I think we need to part ways. I just don't know her anymore. I just can't get close to her at all," Steve complained to his friend, Jeff. They were sipping a beer after another argument with Mila ended in slamming doors, and the two sped off in opposite directions.

Only four weeks later, Steve packed his bags and moved out. He witnessed her having flashbacks of a horrific event. It was a horrible sight to see. She was sweating and shivering, and her eyes looked bewildered. He begged her to allow him to take her for the necessary care. She accused him of being a predator and said that she hated him. He knew that Mila needed help. But she wasn't ready to receive it yet, and he couldn't afford to be hurt by her behavior any longer.

SIGNS AND SYMPTOMS OF CPTSD

Steve had no idea what Mila went through before she and her family became refugees, nor when they first arrived in the country. However, his lack of knowledge of this time in her life wasn't due to his lack of interest. No, he has asked her countless times. It was much rather due to Mila avoiding the time and refusing to share her memories. This type of avoidance is just one of the symptoms of CPTSD, a mental health concern Steve didn't even know existed.

While PTSD and CPTSD do have several overlapping symptoms:

- avoidance behavior

- being in a constant state of high alert

- a lack of trust in others

- insomnia

- dizziness and nausea whenever memories from this traumatic time surface

- being convinced that the world is a horrible place

That said, there are several symptoms that those suffering from the effect of CPTSD on their lives also have to face.

A NEGATIVE SELF IMAGE

Survivors of the trauma linked to CPTSD tend to see themselves as weak failures. They tend to be immersed in shame, worthlessness, and guilt. It is common for them to take the blame for what has happened to them.

FACING CHALLENGES TO FORM AND MAINTAIN RELATIONSHIPS

As we can see in Mila and Steve's story, their relationship was short-lived. It was evident that Mila had no sense of what it meant to trust another person, how to love another, or how to be loved. While Mila's father died in the war in her country, Steve knew her mother and younger brother had come over with her. Yet, she never introduced him to them.

This, too, is typical behavior of someone battling CPTSD. Maintaining relationships is simply too hard when dealing with so much emotional turbulence and internal uncertainty.

EXCESSIVE REACTIONS TO NEGATIVE EMOTIONAL STIMULI

Due to the prolonged exposure to trauma, the attribute setting it apart from the type of situation causing PTSD, those battling CPTSD finds it immensely difficult to manage their emotions. It is common to see an excessively negative response to even the most insignificant stimuli.

DISTORTED PERCEPTIONS OF REALITY

During the time you are exposed to trauma, it is often necessary to shift your perspective to focus on your environment or your abuser just to survive. Prolonged exposure to this state can also create a mental shift where you may become obsessed with revenge, or the complete opposite, feeling responsible for what has happened. Between all these extreme situations, it is hard to recognize reality, and you likely have a distorted perception of what is real.

LACK OF ANY BELIEF SYSTEMS

It isn't only your worldview that can be distorted but also your perception of spirituality or religion. During a traumatic experience, it is normal to feel lonely and hope that someone will come to help you to end the misery. Yet, nobody seems to be coming, and you lose your trust in others, even in the power of spirituality.

DISSOCIATION FROM YOURSELF AND YOUR EMOTIONS

It is common for patients with CPTSD to feel detached from themselves. They experience a detachment from the person they are and how that person is feeling. This perspective on life results from a defense mechanism they have developed to make the trauma they've lived through more bearable.

It is important to remember that these are an overview of the most common symptoms associated with CPTSD and what sets this mental health concern apart from PTSD. However, everyone responds differently to the emotional trauma they've experienced and can portray any combination of the mentioned symptoms.

THE CAUSES OF CPTSD

Three key features set the causes of CPTSD and PTSD apart. The traumatic exposure causing CPTSD was prolonged or repeated over time, and there was no chance of escaping the situation.

Typical situations causing this type of traumatic response are:

- being a victim of or witnessing domestic abuse

- being tortured
- experiencing sexual or physical abuse during childhood years
- witnessing genocide
- being enslaved
- natural disasters and the devastation these events bring
- being a survivor of human trafficking
- being a prisoner of war or living in an area impacted by war
- witnessing the impact of substance abuse in the family
- exposure to neglect or chronic severe poverty
- mental health disorders in the family
- growing up in a high-crime area

Many of these symptoms can be categorized as adverse childhood experiences (ACEs). Statistics indicate that 61% of adults in the United States had exposure to at least one ACE, and one out of every six people in America had exposure to four or more conditions listed as ACEs ("Adverse Childhood Experiences (ACEs)," 2021). Not everyone exposed to these types of traumatic events develops CPTSD, but the more you have been exposed, the higher the odds you'll display the symptoms caused by exposure to such trauma. So, it would be safe to say that the lack of knowledge regarding CPTSD may mean that many people suffering from these symptoms are incorrectly diagnosed or not getting the support and treatment they need.

- Which of these symptoms are you battling daily?

- In this chapter's story, we've learned how both Mila and Steve got hurt due to the symptoms of her CPTSD. Are there people in your life you've hurt unintentionally?

- Are you ready to take the next step to set yourself free to take control of your actions and choices? Or how much longer do you want to remain in your current state?

WHAT HAPPENS IN THE NEUROCHEMISTRY OF THE BRAIN?

Several triggers can spark an onset of the behavior typically linked to CPTSD. Here, we must consider smells, tastes, or sounds that can cause flashbacks. Other triggers are a specific date, month, or season, pain or sensations, and life events like divorce or a breakup. While watching a movie or reading a book, you may encounter things that trigger the mind to recall these memories. As the range of triggers is quite vast and widely spread through everyday life, it should be expected that those dealing with CPTSD will naturally limit their lives substantially to avoid exposure to these triggers.

But what happens in the brain's neurochemistry when exposed to such a trigger?

There are two factors we need to consider when looking at the impact CPTSD has on the brain. The first is the release of neurochemicals once a person is exposed to a trigger. In this case, the most relevant neurochemicals would be those placing the body in the stress or fight or flight response.

These triggers cause a surge in the release of the stress hormones adrenaline and cortisol, placing the body in a high-stress state. Still, it also impacts the secretion of several other neurotransmitters, especially dopamine, serotonin, and norepinephrine. These are only 5 of the more than 40 known neurotransmitters actively involved in mood regulation.

While these chemicals cause various reactions in the body, some changes occur in the brain's shape and structure. The human brain can change shape and size due to neuroplasticity. Neuroplasticity refers to the changes that can happen in a specific brain area when it is more used than others. In the case of CPTSD, the areas of the brain that experience the most changes are the amygdala (pronounced: uh-mig-duh-luh), hippocampus (pronounced: hi-pow-kampuhs), and prefrontal cortex (pronounced: pree-fruhn-tuhl-kaw-teks).

The amygdala is an area located toward the brain's center and is about the size and shape of an almond. While small, it is powerful and is the center where fear and other emotions are processed.

The hippocampus is the center for memory and learning, and for those with CPTSD, it is where memories of traumatic experiences are stored. It is also where we'll find the learned behavior to survive the ordeal, behavior reflecting as symptoms of CPTSD at a later stage.

The prefrontal cortex is in charge of the body's executive functions, which are personality, decision-making, social behavior, and planning. A muscle that is worked in the gym increases in size, shape, and strength; similarly, these areas also expand in size and density. Due to regular exposure to severe conditions and traumatic events, these areas can become overdeveloped compared to other areas in the brain.

These are the physical changes and activities taking place in the brain due to exposure to emotional triggers. Before concluding there is one more distinction we need to make and that is the difference between the conscious mind and the subconscious mind.

With CPTSD, the subconscious mind gets triggered by emotional stressors, but what does this mean?

THE CONSCIOUS MIND AND THE SUBCONSCIOUS MIND

The conscious mind is the location for active thinking to occur. Here you'll plan your future, your next holiday, or even your daily schedule. Every action in the conscious mind is rational, as this is the center of logical thinking.

The subconscious mind is the management center for involuntary actions, habits, and sticking to routines. When you get up in the morning, brush your teeth, have your coffee, and shower to get ready for work, you no longer think about what to do next. No, you've completed this routine so many times your brain is no longer tasking the conscious mind to make these decisions. So, your subconscious mind takes control. That said, it isn't the only action this part of the mind is tasked with, as it is also responsible for involuntary movements.

Under involuntary actions, we can consider breathing, memory, digestion, blood pressure, heart rate, and even attitude. The subconscious mind doesn't seek new information and only operates on what it is provided with.

So, when the brain releases a bunch of stress hormones, placing the body on high alert due to exposure to specific triggers, the subconscious mind reacts by instigating a range of physical responses, causing a high-stress state. As this mind doesn't request new information, there is no consideration of whether these stressors are merely triggers or real. It just assumes that everything it is exposed to is real.

It is how the subconscious mind unknowingly keeps the person dealing with CPTSD trapped until there is an active effort to improve their condition. It is also quite common for patients to express that they are constantly aware of an error lingering somewhere in their subconscious mind. This is why dealing with everyday triggers when you have CPTSD is such a challenge as the brain can consider various physical and emotional stimuli as triggers for an emotional response over which you may have no or limited control.

We'll dig deeper in every chapter and explore the efforts you can make to improve your state and reclaim control over your life. By taking the necessary steps, you can free yourself from the grip CPTSD has on your life.

QUICK RECAP

In many ways, CPTSD manifests in the same manner as PTSD, but there are also vast differences between the two mental health concerns. Of the two, CPTSD is excessively destructive to self-esteem and relationships. What makes it even harder to deal with is that the neurological responses causing the undesired behavior linked to CPTSD take place in the subconscious mind. So, the mind is only relying on the information it is fed and never seeks to validate whether the impulses are real.

Yet, you're not powerless in this situation and there are ways to improve your life so that you can effectively manage your CPTSD. Are you ready to make this shift, to challenge yourself so that you can transform your life? If so, meet me in the next chapter.

3

REORDERING YOUR NEURAL NETWORK AND PATHWAYS

Your brain—every brain—is a work in progress. It is 'plastic.' From the day we're born to the day we die. It continuously revises and remodels, improving or slowly declining, as a function of how we use it. –Michael Merzenich

Neuroplasticity is the best hope for those with mental challenges or a brain injury. The term refers to the brain's inherent ability to change shape, grow denser in certain areas, and adopt new habits, to name only a few of the outcomes you can achieve by using this feature to your advantage. Let's jump into a visualization exercise to make the concept of neuroplasticity easier to understand.

Picture a forest with a pathway leading from one side of the forest to the other. There is only one pathway, so traffic is pretty much limited to flow in one way from one point to another. Even though travelers can move in both ways; their perspective of the forest and their surroundings is limited, and if a tree falls over the pathway, they'll be stuck for a while.

The foliage next to the path is thick, and nobody ever steps off the path as they don't know what lies beyond the natural barriers they're so familiar with. So, the path remains a clear area carrying regular traffic. This has been the case for the longest time, but then the people living in villages around the forest decide to find shorter pathways to get direct access to all the villages, depending on their chosen path. So, they begin to veer off the path, and by moving through the forest in different directions, they begin to form new tracks.

As these pathways are now used primarily, they have been widened by the traffic they carry. The original path is now used less often, causing some of the natural growth to return, and gradually it doesn't stand out any longer as there is now a network of pathways going through the forest. This eases traffic and dramatically shortens the time it takes to travel from one town to another, as there are many options to choose from.

In the brain, there are specific neuron pathways we tend to use often. These have been formed by past experiences, memories, events, and outcomes. These may be the clear pathways and the preferred road for all neurons, delivering similar results every time. But once you learn a new skill or take any action to form new neuron pathways, the structure of the brain changes and this ability to change is referred to as neuroplasticity.

When battling CPTSD, your brain also needs new neuron pathways, as the existing paths keep the challenges you're battling with alive. You can rely on medication and psychotherapy to create these pathways in your brain.

WHY YOU SHOULD OPT FOR A COMBINATION OF MEDICATION AND PSYCHOTHERAPY

Regarding medication and psychotherapy, it is essential to realize that both can be used to improve your mental state, but you can enjoy optimal results when you combine the two. So, rather than weighing up your options of which one you should choose, let's explore the benefits you can enjoy from settling for both.

The first argument many have against using both solutions is the cost of paying for two types of treatment. Sure, this can be an expensive course of action, but when you calculate the expense over the long run, it actually works out more affordable to have the initial larger expense. This is due to the next benefit of using both options.

Medication brings a much faster relief to the symptoms you experience. As you'll already be in a better mental space, you can focus your energy on your therapy, ensuring faster improvement. It also means that you'll likely have to attend fewer sessions, which is where the real cost benefit comes in.

In some instances, psychotherapy won't deliver the desired outcome, and therefore, the lack of medication will stall progress and may even add a sense of hopelessness to the existing situation.

So, whether you're leaning more toward taking medication or are more prone to opt for psychotherapy, I urge you to consider adding both options to your treatment plan. Medication will relieve your symptoms instantly and improve your mental state to respond better to your therapy, but psychotherapy will address the cause and equip you with the tools to maintain your mental health.

DIFFERENT TREATMENT OPTIONS

There are different types of psychotherapy available to choose from. I want to highlight two of these: eye movement desensitization and reprocessing (EMDR) and cognitive behavioral therapy (CBT).

WHAT EYE MOVEMENT DESENSITIZATION AND REPROCESSING CAN DO FOR YOU

EMDR is a trusted type of psychotherapy that enables people to recover from the impact of long-term emotional distress on their lives. What sets EMDR apart is that it is a type of therapy that brings about speedy results compared to other forms of psychotherapy, and it proves the assumption that long-term trauma takes time to heal wrong. It also proves that the mind can heal like the body does when injured. This is, of course, possible due to neuroplasticity.

We can compare mental injury caused by long-term exposure to trauma, like in the case of CPTSD, with a wound that is repeatedly poked with a sharp object. For as long as this continues, the wound will never heal and may even get infected. Once the sharp object is no longer impacting the wound, it can begin to heal.

So, what does EMDR entail? This mental health treatment technique relies on eye movement while processing traumatic memories. It is a relatively new type of therapy, dating back to 1989.

This type of therapy is different from many other types of treatment in the sense that it doesn't require patients to talk about their traumatic experiences. It rather addresses these concerns by changing the emotions that surface when these memories are recalled. Therapists can support the brain's healing process through EMDR, by relying on neuroplasticity.

During the first stage of the treatment, the mental health professional will determine which memory they need to use as their starting point for this type of treatment. Next, they'll ask clients to recall these specific memories and hold them in their thoughts while they're following the therapist's hand moving in their field of vision. Using this process, it becomes possible to attach new meaning to specific memories and bring about healing in the client's brain. An example of an outcome that can be established through EDMR would be when a victim of prolonged sexual abuse during childhood no longer considers themselves worthless and instead of thinking that they've deserved this horrendous treatment they start to see themselves as survivors of an unfair ordeal, something that made them stronger. Does this sound like the solution you need?

While EMDR has earned a reputation for being a highly effective treatment, it doesn't mean it will deliver the same results for all. No, you owe it to yourself to research the available treatment options in your area to determine which would be the most effective for you. Everyone has a unique combination of needs and challenges, and in the same manner, unique solutions to address each of these challenges. Yet, the biggest challenge remains in finding the solution that best suits your needs. Are you willing to take on the challenge so that you can heal from within and engage in a fulfilling life?

Another highly recommended treatment option is cognitive behavioral therapy. Let's see what that is all about and how it can help you.

HOW COGNITIVE BEHAVIORAL THERAPY CAN HELP YOU HEAL

Over the years, cognitive behavioral therapy (CBT) has gained a reputation for being a trusted aid in recovery from depression, anxiety, eating disorders, and even drug and alcohol abuse. It brings about significant improvement in a range of mental health challenges. The success of CBT is rooted in the following principles: It claims that all psychological problems originate in unhelpful ways of thinking or unhelpful learned behavior. It also states that everyone can learn better ways to cope with their symptoms and so empower themselves to live effective, happy, and satisfying lives.

CBT utilizes several techniques to change a certain way of thinking by instilling a new perspective on what motivates others and what determines their behavior. It touches on problem-solving skills, improves confidence, and eliminates distorted thinking. You can also prepare yourself for possible role play and to learn skills that help you face your fears and relax and quiet your mind.

The foundation of CBT is to prepare every client to become their own therapist, making it much easier to sustain mental health and enjoy lasting results. If this is the type of therapy you consider, be prepared for homework, but know that every exercise will contribute to your healing and prepare you to take control of your mental health.

As CBT is focused on changing unhealthy ways of thinking and behavioral patterns, it has proven to be a highly effective approach to giving relief to patients suffering from CPTSD. This type of therapy can change deep-rooted thinking patterns and beliefs that keep you mentally captured even when the trauma you've experienced is over. It is a treatment option that can utilize neuroplasticity in such an effective manner that it can change errors in thinking. For example, it can minimize your negative perceptions about a specific situation and help bring the positive aspects to the foreground. Until your perspective on the world and your life is aligned with reality.

Due to these benefits associated with CBT, many of the exercises and strategies discussed in this book are based on

CBT and its methods. As one of the desired outcomes of CBT is to enable clients to take responsibility for their mental health by providing them with the necessary tools to do so, there is a lot that can be learned from this type of therapy. These are the strategies I present to you to help you kit out your mental health toolbox in a manner that empowers you, now and in the future.

NEUROPLASTICITY GIVES HOPE

What is hope? Hope is the belief that things will improve. It may not be today or tomorrow and not without effort or investing your time, but it can and will improve. What hope does is it gives back power to the hopeless. It encourages them to persevere on their journey to enjoy a better life. It brings light where there is only darkness.

When you're battling mental health challenges, neuroplasticity brings about that hope. It is what can keep you going when your current situation becomes overwhelming. The mere knowledge that your brain can change and that there are tools to establish this change, medication, and psychotherapy, to name only some, brings hope to many. That, and the many success stories told by those who once found themselves in the dark place you may be at right now.

That said, it is not only these types of therapies that bring new memories but also new experiences, new skills, and the opportunity to gain new perspectives on your life that can reshape your brain, and so also your perspective on the world.

THE SERENITY PRAYER

Are you familiar with the words of the serenity prayer? The prayer is about searching for wisdom to distinguish between things you can change and those you can't. It asks for the courage to change the things within your control and the ability to make peace with the matters you have no control over to find internal peace.

> God grant me the serenity.
>
> To accept the things I cannot change;
>
> Courage to change the things I can;
>
> And wisdom to know the difference.
>
> Living one at a time;
>
> Enjoying one moment at a time;
>
> Accepting hardships as the pathway to peace; ("Serenity Prayer – Applying 3 Truths from the Bible," 2022, para 8 - 9).

This prayer isn't tied to religion. It is the prayer often linked to Alcoholics Anonymous. It calls for wisdom and understanding so you don't lose hope. So that you don't waste your limited energy and time or any other resources on matters you have no control over.

I understand you may feel powerless, tired, controlled, hopeless, and vulnerable as you stand here. I also grasp that you may not feel like you have the strength to establish healing in your life and that you're ready to give up. Yet, I want you to hold on, to be strong.

You can't change the past. You can't do anything to undo what has happened to you. You can't change others or how they perceive you. But you do have control over your future and where you're heading. You can create a life so far removed from what you're enduring now. Let's progress by taking the first steps in the right direction to claim your control and set you free. Meet me in the next chapter as our journey continues.

- What are the biggest obstacles in your way right now?
- Are these matters you have control over?

Identify the things you have control over, and let's determine how you can make the most of these to overcome the obstacles keeping you from living the life you deserve.

QUICK RECAP

The brain may have suffered physical injury or emotional trauma, leaving it wounded, bruised, and even mutilated in a sense. But there is hope. Just like a cut on your skin will heal naturally, so will the injuries you've suffered also heal. All you need is the correct treatment options, perfectly suited to address your unique concerns. The brain can form new pathways, make new memories, change perspectives, and link new meaning to old perceptions. This ability is called neuroplasticity.

Through a combination of medication and therapy, you can help your brain to heal. While medication may bring immediate relief to your symptoms and support a more balanced state, therapy serves as a tool to change perspectives, adopt new skills, and uncover truths about the range of your control over your life. Two of the most prominent therapeutic options are EMDR and CBT, but I encourage you to expand your vision to find the treatment option that is the best fit for you.

You can't change the past but can change the future by taking the necessary steps today.

4

RECOVERING FROM CPTSD BY UNDERSTANDING TRAUMA

It is during our darkest moments that we must focus to see the light. –Aristotle

What often makes a traumatic experience so traumatic is that it happens quite unexpectedly. That, and the fact that the mind builds more trauma on top of what has already happened.

GINA'S STORY

Gina was in the wrong place at the wrong time. That was what her brother told everyone.

It all happened only three weeks after she moved to the city, hoping to bid small-town living goodbye once and for all. But her excitement over this huge step she was taking was about more than leaving her roots to spread her wings. She also got accepted into a prestigious school for young designers. It was her opportunity to build a name for herself, to shape her future.

It was the Friday of her first week at the fashion academy when she decided to work slightly later to get a head-start on one of her designs. When she walked to the subway, she realized it was somewhat darker than usual, which made her put a bit more speed into her steps.

When she took her seat on the subway, she thought how silly she was to be scared, as she could now see that the city was perfectly safe, or at least on her route. She was still looking at the other passengers, and as she wasn't traveling during peak time, there were not enough people to properly take time to look at them all, but then she got distracted. Her phone rang. It was her mom. The two had a lovely chat, as they always do, but when the call ended, Gina realized she missed her stop. Frantically she got off at the next stop, only to realize this wasn't a good neighborhood.

Walking down the street, now already much darker, she doubted whether she should get back onto the train instead of walking home the entire time. After about 10 minutes, she returned to the subway, but now the station was almost empty. She was waiting for the next train when she heard a noise. It was when she noticed a couple of youngsters coming downstairs. They were arguing. She still couldn't explain why, but she immediately felt the need to hide. Yes, to remain out of sight until the next train stops. From her position behind a pillar, she could see them. The argument got fiercer, and then one pulled out a gun.

He was blind with rage. Gina still didn't know what it was all about. Now the entire crowd was screaming at one person, and the gunman took the end of the weapon and hit the other one in the face. He fell down. Blood was dripping. He was begging. The gun was pointed at his head. She was holding her breath, her heart racing. She didn't want to see it happen but still couldn't stop watching. It got worse and worse. She could hear the train coming. Louder and louder. It entered the subway. The shot echoed above the noise of the train. She screamed. The doors opened. She ran. They saw her. The doors closed. The train pulled away. She was safe. But it didn't feel that way.

This happened three months ago, but for Gina, it remains real every night in her dreams. Her sleep is disturbed by images of the man's face begging for mercy, his eyes looking straight at her, pleading for her to scream. Danny McCallister was his name, or so the article reporting on the subway murder stated. He was 19, her age. There was nothing she could do. Yet she still feels guilty, edgy, and scared. She has missed so many classes since the event she got expelled. She didn't tell anyone at school or go to the police as she was scared of what might happen to her. She hasn't made any friends in the city yet, and as she was avoiding the streets and being social, she was lonely. Her parents came to pack up her things and took her home, but it didn't get better there either. She refused to get help or to talk about what she saw to anyone. But she can't forget what she saw.

Even far from the crime scene, she remains scared and startles easily at home. She feels guilty and suffers from panic attacks. She lost her appetite for food and life. As her parents need to leave every day to work, she is alone at home. Here she stays in her bed most of the time. Thinking about what happened, her mind adds more detail, exaggerating the moment and worsening her trauma.

Gina is a victim of a traumatic experience. The nature of the event, being a once-off occurrence that she could escape, doesn't qualify as CPTSD, but she is showing symptoms that she is suffering in the aftermath of a traumatic experience.

FIVE SIGNS YOU'VE BEEN THROUGH TRAUMA

Traumatic experiences manifest in victims in several ways and can affect every aspect of their health.

- The psychological impact includes persistent, overwhelming fear, depression, shame, obsessive-compulsive behavior, anger, anxiety, and even panic attacks.

- On a physical level, expect edginess, insomnia, sexual dysfunction, a loss of appetite, inexplicable aches and pains, and being easily startled.

- Due to these challenges, you can also expect behavioral changes, confusion, mood swings, nightmares, memory loss, and mood swings.

- Trauma is also associated with emotional challenges like being trapped in a state of disbelief or shock over what you've witnessed, being scared that what you've seen can happen to you, or if it was you it happened to, that the event will repeat itself. You don't have anywhere safe to go. It can also go along with a sense of sadness and grief.

- This type of behavior will put stress on your relationships and make it harder to sustain them, even to the point where there may be a complete breakdown of bonds.

These symptoms can surface directly after the traumatic event or manifest only during the following days or weeks. Usually, these symptoms only last for a couple of weeks, but in some cases, like in Gina's case, these symptoms can last much longer. The duration of these concerns depends on how severe the experience was and whether there is sufficient emotional support. Personality types and familiarity with coping mechanisms are also influential factors determining how long recovery will take.

THE BRAIN'S RESPONSE TO TRAUMA

The first step toward recovery is understanding what exactly you're up against. When it is trauma that you are combating, it is essential to understand how trauma affects the brain, as this will determine how it will impact your life.

The first and likely most important factor to consider is that the brain doesn't respond to trauma in the same way as it would to any other event. It doesn't store traumatic memories in the same way it would keep memories of how you had fun at a birthday party a few weeks ago. No, when it comes to trauma, the brain captures images of the traumatic experience and stores these in the amygdala as sensory fragments. In simpler terms, it means that the brain doesn't store your memories of the event as images but as experiences or sensations captured through the five senses. Gina's memories of the traumatic event aren't only centered around what she saw, but what she remembers is the coldness of the tiled pillar against her back while she was hiding out of sight, the smell of urine in the subway, the feeling of the seat on the subway when she clenched her fingers into the soft inner, and the taste of vomit in her mouth when she got sick the moment she got off at the next stop.

However, her memories also include the image of the victim's eyes looking at her helplessly. Yet, she was never close enough to see his expression with such vividness as she remembers. This brings me to the second important fact about how the brain processes trauma. It adds to the memories, making it worse than it was. No, you're not exaggerating the events on purpose. What is happening is quite a normal process and beyond your control. But it is helpful to acknowledge that this is taking place. As if the traumatic experience wasn't terrible enough, your brain will continue to color it in, making it even more horrible than it was. Therefore, it is best to capture your memories in words as soon as possible afterward, as this will help you identify variations of your memories that may occur later.

Consider the last traumatic event you've witnessed. How much of your memories are based on reality, and what are figments of your brain's overeager approach to crochet together an even more traumatic event? This reaction towards traumatic events is also evident when a crowd has witnessed a traumatic event. If you ask each individual what they saw, there will undoubtedly be many aspects of the story that correspond between them, but there will also be many variations. Everyone will have a slightly different version of what they've seen as the brain convinces you that you've seen things differently than they were.

HOW TO OVERCOME TRAUMA

The better equipped you are with a range of coping mechanisms to overcome the effect of trauma in your life, the sooner you'll free yourself from the impact the event had on you. The following strategies all constitute easy but effective ways to overcome these effects.

LEARN AS MUCH AS POSSIBLE ABOUT YOUR TRAUMA

It is important to get what you've witnessed out of your system, for every time you talk about it, your mind is processing the memories of what happened. It is why it is so vital to identify your support network and to share your story as many times as you can. A support network can include family and friends, a formal support group, or mental health care professionals. You can also write about your feelings, what you've witnessed, and how it affected your life. Use any means you have to get more familiar with what you've been exposed to, as through familiarity, the event will lose its sting, and how it disrupted your life will gradually ease out.

- Have you been exposed to a traumatic event?

- Have you identified your support network to talk to?

- If you haven't captured the event details yet, do so now. An easy way to get started is to report what happened as if you're a journalist writing about the event for your local paper. This will help you to work through the facts of what has happened.

- Was it a once-off event, or did you experience repeated exposure?

- If it was repeated exposure, consider that what you're dealing with is likely not trauma but CPTSD.

IDENTIFY WHAT YOU'RE FEELING

What emotions did the event cause you to feel? Remember that your feelings can change over time and may even vary from day to day. Don't deny your feelings or judge yourself for what you're feeling. Instead, acknowledge and accept these emotions as part of the recovery process.

- Identify and list the emotions you're having.

- Have these feelings changed over time?

CONNECT WITH YOUR BEHAVIORAL CHANGES ASSOCIATED WITH THE TRAUMA

You're bound to experience certain changes in your behavior due to what you've been through. Here too, remember to be kind to yourself. Allow sufficient time for self-care, as you need to look after yourself right now. It can be easy to get so consumed by your thoughts and fears that you neglect to care for even your most basic needs. So, take time to spend in nature, exercise, rest, and maintain a healthy diet.

- Determine how the feelings you've listed in the previous exercise are affecting your behavior.

- Have you shared what has happened to you with others affected by your behavior?

AVOID SUBSTANCES KEEPING YOU FROM CONNECTING WITH YOUR PAIN

It is common for people who were exposed to trauma to desperately suppress their memories. By choosing this way out, you're putting yourself at risk of prolonging the impact trauma has on your life, as it is vital to confront and process your memories of the event and how it makes you feel. However, the most prominent concern is rooted in the fact that the easiest way to suppress these memories is through substance abuse. Both alcohol and other substances will place you in a state where these memories become vague. But you're making yourself vulnerable to addiction, for every time the effect of these substances wears off, you'll be confronted again with the same challenges as if you aren't processing the event constructively. So, the need to drown your memories persists, keeping you hooked.

- Are you already relying on alcohol or any other substance to ease the pain you're feeling?

- Commit to replacing this habit by taking more productive steps to support your recovery.

QUICK RECAP

Exposure to trauma can place your life at a complete standstill, but it doesn't have to derail your entire future like it did in Gina's case. There are several steps you can take to make recovery easier and faster. A lot of the success you'll enjoy in recovering from the impact of such an event depends on how you approach the memories and feelings you're dealing with after the event.

The first step would be to identify what you're feeling and whether the changes in your life are caused by a traumatic event. Once you know what you're dealing with and why, it becomes much easier to take the necessary steps to overcome the psychological obstacles caused by what happened to you or what you've witnessed. However, consider the difference between dealing with the aftermath of traumatic exposure and overcoming the hurdles CPTSD presents. Next, we will explore several steps you can take in greater detail.

5

HEALING CPTSD BY WORKING ON YOUR BODY

Your mind, emotions and body are instruments and the way you align and tune them determines how well you play life. –Harbhajan Singh Yogi

While 9,2% of veterans suffer from coronary heart disease, only 4,7% of non-veterans battle the same health concern (Hinojosa, 2018). The veterans also experienced a substantially higher rate of heart conditions, strokes, and heart attacks. These results were captured during a 2018 study by Ramon Hinojosa including 150,000 veteran and non-veteran participants to identify significant differences in the two groups' health challenges.

These results may be shocking initially, but they are, in fact, perfectly aligned with what can be expected from long-term exposure to traumatic events, typical to the events synonymous with combat. However, these aren't health concerns only veterans experience, as anyone with CPTSD is at risk of facing similar health concerns due to the way mental health challenges impact the body. This is an impact predominantly resulting from long-term exposure to a high-stress state. But to fully comprehend the connection between CPTSD on the body, we need to shift our focus right from the start to initial exposure to the first traumatic event.

CPTSDS CONNECTION WITH THE BODY

The mind-body connection is one of immense complexity as these two systems are intrinsically infused. Therefore, any traumatic experience will impact the body too. So, let's start at the very beginning to see how the mind affects the body.

When initial exposure to trauma occurs, the nervous system activates the limbic system to release a surge of stress hormones that activate several systems in the body to prepare it to fight or flee. The process is referred to as the stress response but also often goes by the name of the fight or flight response.

The limbic system may release a range of stress hormones or neurochemicals, preparing the body to enter a state optimal to ensure survival. Still, the two hormones in the spotlight are cortisol and adrenaline.

These hormones trigger a range of physiological changes.

The lung muscles relax to allow more air to enter, while the smallest bronchi open to ease oxygen transfer to the blood, ensuring an optimal supply of oxygen to the muscles.

The person's heart rate picks up to get the blood high in oxygen faster to the necessary muscle groups. While this happens, the veins and artery walls narrow to increase the pressure in the circulatory system. These aren't the only changes taking place in this system, though. No, the same stress hormones also redirect circulation away from systems not contributing to survival in the stress-burdened moment. Blood flow is diverted from the digestive, immune, and reproductive systems. Excess oxygen is transported to the brain to ensure clarity and focus while the pupils open wider, allowing more light into the eyes and enhancing long-distance focus. These changes are regulated by a subdivision of the nervous system called the sympathetic nervous system (SNS).

Once the threat has passed, the parasympathetic nervous system (PSNS) kicks into action. This system is responsible for returning the body to inner calm. It also relies on releasing hormones to convey messages across the body, letting the heart rate slow down and blood pressure drop to normal levels. It tightens the lung muscles to allow for easier breathing. The pupils close up a bit more to allow for easier short-distance focus. Blood circulation is redirected to the digestive, immune, and reproductive systems.

So, this is a perfect system, right? It is intended to save your life and to restore calm. Yet, one of the key features setting CPTSD apart from other threatening or traumatic situations is that exposure to these incidents is repeated. So, there isn't a once-off exposure to trauma, but repeated exposure, for example, during sexual abuse at home. So, the body remains in a high-stress state. While the human body is equipped to deal with high-stress situations, it doesn't do well when this exposure lasts longer, not to even mention when exposure to trauma exceeds days, weeks, months, or even years.

A prolonged high-stress state negatively impacts the body in several ways, but let's start with what it does to the brain. As the body remains stressed for so long, this state becomes the new normal. It means that the trauma you've been exposed to gets trapped inside the body and can rewire the brain due to neuroplasticity. As the brain becomes rewired to remain in this alert state, it impacts your thoughts, behavior, and relationships. These changes manifest in your life as memory lapses, constant alertness, disassociation, and all the other symptoms linked to CPTSD already.

The changes you can expect in the body align with what anyone exposed to prolonged stress will experience. Persistent high blood pressure puts unnecessary strain on the cardiac system, increasing the risk of strokes, heart disease, and heart attacks. This is, of course, what the study mentioned earlier witnessed in veterans.

As circulation is diverted from the digestive system, you'll experience poor digestion, a lack of appetite, constipation or diarrhea, and even diabetes. A lack of sufficient support to the immune system increases the chances of getting sick, while the same lack in the reproductive system causes a lack of libido.

- What are the physical symptoms you're experiencing due to CPTSD?

- How are these symptoms holding you back in life?

- Are you trapped in a cycle where CPTSD is harming your health while your physical state is adding to your emotional challenges?

- Are you ready to do something about it?

I hope you are ready to proceed to the next stage where you'll be able to actively work toward holistic improvement and that you're motivated to reclaim your life by taking a few small, regular steps.

WHY YOU NEED TO WORK WITH YOUR BODY TO IMPROVE THE IMPACT OF CPTSD

Mental conditions impact the body. The good news is that you can, and should, use your body to improve the impact your mental state has on your overall health.

You can use various calming techniques to significantly improve your mental state. I am referring here specifically to practices like breathing exercises, mindfulness meditation, and any other form of exercise. Physical activity increases the release of feel-good hormones that help reduce stress levels, but the other practices mentioned also bring about a heightened state of relaxation.

Grounding exercises also help to improve the symptoms of anxiety and panic attacks. So, by working with your body, you can enjoy immediate relief from unbearable symptoms.

Body scanning is another technique that delivers instant improvement in your physical and mental states. Something as simple as breathing exercises can help to activate that PSNS, instructing the brain to flip the switch between being in a stressed state controlled by the SNS and moving into a state of calm managed by the PSNS.

While mentioning the PSNS and the SNS, let's pause for a moment to explore these two systems in greater depth.

UNDERSTANDING THE SYSTEMS CONTROLLING STRESS LEVELS

So, by now, you know that the SNS triggers the stress response while the PSNS initiates and manages a state of inner calm.

Both these systems form part of the autonomic nervous system. The latter is the part of the nervous system controlling involuntary processes. Clapping your hands, walking, and texting are all voluntary or deliberate processes. You've consciously decided to take these action steps, but you don't think about the many functions necessary to keep you alive and well. Blood pressure, temperature control, digestion, oxygen transfer to the lungs, and immune defense are only some of the many behind-the-scenes actions necessary to live a healthy and happy life. They are mostly forgotten until you experience some failure that causes health concerns. These are the actions controlled by the autonomic nervous system, a system we can divide into smaller distinct divisions: the PSNS and the SNS. The SNS is the system in charge of the stress response, and the PSNS is critical to return to a calm state.

HOW TO USE YOUR BODY

You can apply several techniques to work with your body to establish the desired change.

PROGRESSIVE RELAXATION

Progressive muscle relaxation (PMR) was developed by Edmund Jacobson, an American physician, during the 1920s. He based this type of relaxation exercise on the principle that you can increase mental calm and physical relaxation by following a series of stretch and relaxation exercises. His technique of stressing and relaxing your muscles has become a widely known technique to use your body to improve your mental state and combat the impact of CPTSD.

The key is to work with one muscle group at a time. The practical steps are:

1. Find a comfortable position, sitting or lying on your back, where you can spend about 15-20 minutes undisturbed.

2. Start by taking a couple of deep breaths.

3. Then begin at one point of your body, preferably the toes, and stress your toes. Stretch them forward, upward, or downward and hold the stretch for about five counts before releasing the stress and moving into a relaxed state.

4. Move on to your feet and ankles and do the same.

5. Then, move on to the calf muscles. Stretch them and relax.

6. When you get to your buttock, clench them together and relax.

7. Then you can stretch your fingers by spreading them open, hold for five counts, and relax.

8. Move up all the way in your arms.

9. Stretch your back, clench your abdomen muscles, hold for five counts, and relax.

10. When you get to your shoulders, pull them upwards toward your ears, hold, and relax.

11. When you get to your face, you can pout your lips, clench your eyelids, lift your brows, hold the position for about five counts, and relax.

12. Once you've worked your way through from your toes to your crown, notice how much more relaxed your body is and the increased sense of calm in the mind.

13. Take a couple of deep breaths and continue with your day.

14. Repeat this routine daily to enjoy instant relief and lasting improvement in the challenges you're facing,

as the process of deliberate relaxation will encourage the PSNS to react.

MASSAGE

The symptoms of trauma and stress don't only get trapped in the brain but also in the body's tissue, like its muscles. During a massage, muscles are manipulated to relax, and pressure on the muscles improves circulation in those areas. It means receiving a better supply of oxygen and nutrients while toxins are released to be flushed out of the system.

Massage and this type of manipulation of the muscles decrease the level of the stress hormone cortisol and increase serotonin levels. It means the hormonal balance is restored to ensure greater emotional and physical wellness. The immensity of the emotions released during such a session can sometimes reach the point where you may sigh, twitch, or even cry as deep-rooted emotions surface.

This ancient therapy is known for reducing stress and anxiety and serving as an effective treatment for depression. It can be a helpful step to include in your plan directed toward recovery and therefore deserves thorough consideration as a way to work with the body to improve your symptoms.

You'll need to book the services of a qualified massage therapist, but there are specific steps you can take before your session to ensure your mind and body gain optimal results.

- Take a hot shower to increase circulation in advance.
- Be sure to stay hydrated as your body needs to flush out the toxins through the kidneys once released from your muscles.
- Dress comfortably.
- Prepare yourself mentally for the process focused on relaxation and healing.
- During the massage, communicate your needs to the therapist.
- Maintain a relaxed state.

MEDITATION

Meditation is a practice that has been around for centuries. It plays an immense role in different religions, spirituality, and healthy living. It is based on your ability to quiet your mind by focusing on only one object while establishing a state of deep physical relaxation through breathing exercises.

There are many types of meditation, and I encourage you to try a few types to find the kind of meditation that works best for you. That said, I am sharing the steps to mindfulness meditation, a technique known to bring about a great sense of physical relaxation and mental calmness, and is easy to follow. You'll be able to experience instant relief but also gradually train your brain to take better control of your thoughts, ensuring improved management to keep your mind from drifting off to negative images and flashbacks of what happened in the past.

It may be helpful to book a guided meditation session for your first couple of sessions to help and encourage you to improve. You can also download many of the available apps offering this type of support or follow the following steps on your own.

1. Find a place where you can remain undisturbed for a couple of minutes.

2. Set a timer for how long you want to meditate. Five minutes will be a good start, but try to extend these sessions as you get better at it.

3. Make sure you are wearing comfortable clothes.

4. Sit in a comfortable position. It can be cross-legged or any other position you're comfortable in and remain in for a while. It may also help to sit on a cushion to avoid distracting discomfort during your session.

5. Relax your body and mind by breathing in and out deeply a couple of times.

6. Close your eyes and set your intention for what you want to achieve during this session.

7. Now, shift your focus to your breathing.

8. Take note of the air as it passes through your airways and fills your lungs. Take note of your chest opening up wide, expanding, and your belly pushing up to allow the life-giving air to enter your body.

9. Exhale slowly and visualize how all the stress, anxiety, upsetting thoughts, and memories exit your body.

10. Repeat this type of breathing for as long as your session lasts.

11. When your mind wanders off, gradually recognize that it happened and return to focusing on your breathing.

Once you are done, be grateful for these couple of minutes spent connecting with mind and body, notice your greater sense of calm, and commit to making this a regular practice.

POLYVAGAL EXERCISES

To understand how polyvagal exercises work, we must shift our focus to the SNS and PSNS again. To be precise, these systems are part of the *automatic* nervous system. When you're combating the impact of CPTSD on your life, your body is in a state of disarray, but you can restore balance by healing the nervous system through these exercises.

The theory on polyvagal exercises states that the Vagus nerve, part of the autonomic nervous system, detects signals of danger from your surroundings, placing the body in a stressed state. But it is also alert to signs indicating safety and calm from the surrounding. Yet, if the body remains in a state of stress for too long, like with the type of exposure causing CPTSD, it is hard for the body to shift back to a calm state. Through these exercises, you can encourage your body to step out of stress to improve your physiological state. Social interaction depends on invoking a sense of security and shifting the mind from its primitive response of fight or flight to experiencing greater freedom and being social. As supportive tips, it also relies on self-care and being kind to yourself.

Under the umbrella term of polyvagal exercises, we find quite a wide range of options, including deep breathing exercises, similar to what you would use in mindfulness meditation, closed exhalation, and even applying cold water to your body. But let's explore a couple of these options in greater detail.

APPLYING COLD WATER TO THE BODY

Yes, I want to start expanding on these options as it is a simple way to use your body to improve your mental state. You can activate the Vagus nerve by splashing cold water onto your body. When you do, it slows down the activity of the SNS, which is keeping you in a stressed state and activates the PSNS to restore calmness.

VOCALIZATION

This exercise is effective due to the location of the Vagus nerve, right between the vocal cords and the inner ear. By humming, singing, or even gargling, your vocal cords vibrate, stimulating the Vagus nerve into action and restoring a state of relaxation and inner calm. It is why making the "om" sound is common when meditating.

Working with your body can be as easy and simple as the above exercises, but you can also go into it more deeply. It depends on you, but I recommend that you start small but stick to continuous exercises, and gradually, you'll notice improvement.

QUICK RECAP

The mind and body are way too integrated not to expect that one will impact the other. That said, as mind and body are so infused into each other, we can use and work with the body to create a state of mental calmness and physical relaxation to benefit our health and wellness. Yes, just as your mental state can harm your health, as we've seen from the statistics from the studies exploring the health of veterans' health, we can use the body to flip the switch on stress by activating the PSNS to ensure homeostasis.

Another essential factor is that improvement is possible when turning our focus from within to our immediate environment. Who are the people you surround yourself with? How can emotional support benefit you? This is the topic we'll explore next.

6

HEALING CPTSD THROUGH EMOTIONAL SUPPORT

Traumatized people chronically feel unsafe inside their bodies: The past is alive in the form of gnawing interior discomfort. –Bessel van der Kolk

The choice to isolate is one of the key symptoms linked to CPTSD. This is often due to our inability to shut the past off. For those suffering from CPTSD, escaping past trauma seems to be an impossible quest. While you may want to shed these memories as much as you like, it remains what appears to be an impossible quest. Coupled with the inner narrative that you deserved what happened to you, it is common to prefer being alone or not bothered. It is when you start to protect yourself with a shield of isolation. It is not animosity toward others, as it is often wrongfully perceived to be. No, it is merely a safety mechanism to reduce the level of vulnerability you're familiar with daily. That and the fact that you're constantly living in the past, a lonely place, when everyone else you're surrounded with is in the present, pondering about the future.

In contrast to this persistent desire for isolation, emotional support can lead to healing.

JORDAN'S STORY

It was a cold winter's day. A fine rain was gently coming down, leaving tiny water droplets in Jordan's thick blonde mane and on the bridge's railing, which he had already been holding onto for about five minutes. Yet, it felt like he had been holding on to his pain for a lifetime. In many ways, he isn't wrong. For most of his life, 18 years, 5 months, and 4 days, he endured persistent sexual abuse from his stepdad. The abuse left him with aches and pains throughout his entire body. Over time, the pain became too severe for him to handle any longer, and that is how he ended up on the edge of the bridge. Yet, he hasn't jumped, for every time he looked down at the river in flood beneath, a voice in his head told him to get off.

"Hey man!" he heard a voice behind him. The man in the green cardigan startled him, and he almost lost his grip.

"Go away!" Jordan called back.

"It's not worth it, man," the man continued to come nearer.

This drama continued for quite some time until the green cardigan man convinced him to tell his story first before he jumped.

This was a first for Jordan. To open up and share his pain, something he did with much greater ease than he thought he would. But then he realized that it was because he knew he would jump and that none of this mattered anymore. Jordan shared his story, what the monster of a man does to him, how his mother betrays him, knowing what her husband does to her son and not speaking up, how it hurts him, and even how the smell of stale ale makes him instantly vomit, but that he has to swallow it for if he makes a mess, it all just lasts for so much longer. When Jordan was done, he felt lighter, understood for the first time ever, and less inclined to return to the railing. The man in the green cardigan got up and asked if he was cold. "Yes," Jordan said, shivering. Then, the man offered to buy him food, "Let's make it sort of your last meal," he said.

Jordan got up, followed the man to a nearby diner, and never returned to the bridge.

The man in the green cardigan was a professor of psychology at a nearby university. As his wife passed away only a couple of months ago, he had a big empty house and offered that Jordan could stay in a room. Jordan took on the offer, unaware that every conversation with the man was some therapy.

After a couple of months, Jordan got a job at a pizza place. He returned to finish school. He joined support groups the man introduced him to. Here he made friends with people facing similar challenges as he did. They became his support group. A few weeks ago, Jordan's stepdad was finally sentenced. It took Jordan three years and a couple of weeks since he got off the railing to have enough strength and courage to speak up about how he was wronged, but he did so that his stepdad couldn't hurt anyone else again.

Can you identify with Jordan's story?

Have you ever felt entirely suppressed by your emotional burden until you've shared your thoughts, memories, feelings, and fears with another?

Are you familiar with the relief when you reach out to your support network to unburden yourself and gain the necessary support to overcome your challenges?

FIVE REASONS TO FIND EMOTIONAL SUPPORT

People are social beings. Yes, you may be introverted and feel drained after having lots of social interaction, but that is different than being isolated from human interaction entirely. Having meaningful relationships with others is vital to sustain our mental and physical health. We need the emotional support of others in good times and especially during bad times.

There are several benefits to having access to such supportive networks. Benefits that can transform your life if you're battling CPTSD.

1. Several studies have revealed that emotional support is essential in reducing stress and anxiety (Parincu, n.d.). Both anxiety and depression are symptoms of CPTSD, but they are also factors that can worsen the concern and make it even more challenging to deal with daily.

2. It minimizes stress levels. A shared problem is half a problem; when you have someone you can share your concerns with, they become less daunting. You may gain new perspectives on the challenge you're facing, giving you the insight to approach your obstacles from a different angle and the courage to proceed.

3. As emotional support reduces stress, it improves your overall health and well-being by lowering your blood pressure, improving your immune system, taking care of your heart health, and restoring your appetite.

4. Access to an emotional support network you can rely on can even bring longevity. Not only in the way the man in the green cardigan saved Jordan's life since statistics reveal that, on average, longevity increases by 3 years for women and 2,3 years for men (Parincu, n.d.).

5. Through emotional support, you can expand your emotional intelligence and improve your approach to life, your relationships, and the necessary steps you need to take to engage with society and take control of your life.

Do these benefits inspire and motivate you to establish an emotional support network you can rely on?

- Were there times in your life when you did have emotional support?
- How did access to this support benefit you?
- Do you have a support network? List the people you can rely on to be there for you.
- If you don't have a support network, identify people you would like to be part of it.

THE RISKS OF ISOLATION

Due to the reasons discussed earlier, isolation may appear as the safer option when battling the symptoms of CPTSD. But essentially, you're opening yourself up to even more significant possible concerns.

Social isolation severely impacts the mind, and it can devastate your physical health too. Even your cognitive abilities can deteriorate due to social isolation.

Health concerns commonly linked to social isolation include a rapid decline in cognitive abilities, a weakened cardiovascular system, and impaired executive functions. Social isolation is also linked to poor immune response and insomnia (Novotney, n.d.).

It is also a contributing factor to depression. Due to CPTSD, depression is likely already a considerable concern, becoming a problem of even greater magnitude through isolation.

In 2019, a doctor at the American Cancer Society ran a test on more than half a million participants to determine the correlation between social isolation and mortality. The study indicated a significant increase in premature death due to social isolation (Novotney, n.d.).

The lack of social interaction and the necessary emotional support also increases the risk of adopting unhealthy habits like drug or alcohol abuse. People who are isolated and lack essential emotional support are more inclined to have eating disorders.

When you spend most of your time alone, you get more trapped in your mind, allowing your thoughts to keep you trapped. During these times, the brain is working at an advanced pace to intensify the trauma you're experiencing. It is when every traumatic experience you've been exposed to during the past spins out of control that your situation comes across as more helpless than you are. This helps the trauma to stay alive in your mind.

Choosing social isolation naturally also means neglecting your relationships and losing these vital bonds in life.

To capture all of the above in one sentence, we can say that healthy relationships are vital in your recovery and ability to control your life.

HOW TO CREATE A NETWORK FOR HEALING

An emotional support network can be defined as a group of trusted people you can turn to when you need support in any form. This can include family members, friends, formal groups, or mental health professionals. It can also be that you have several support networks that you can tap into when needed. If you find it hard to reach out to others or to ask for support, it will be helpful to know that today there are also many online support groups you can join, making it easier in the sense that you don't have to leave your home and don't have to meet in person with strangers. Like in Jordan's case, it is sometimes easier to share your feelings with strangers, people you know you'll never look in the eye again. So, don't dismiss this support platform before trying it out.

Another way you can reach out to others and form lasting bonds is to volunteer your services. While the focus of volunteering is to help others, you may be surprised to learn how much benefit you can gain from becoming a volunteer. You can always volunteer at an animal shelter if you feel you're not up to facing larger crowds. Animals are great for offering support too. You may even consider getting a pet, like a dog, as your support animal. They may not be able to talk back, but the right puppy or kitty will surely look at you like they listen to every word and, even more importantly, feel your pain.

STAYING ON TOP OF YOUR NEED FOR EMOTIONAL SUPPORT

You know that all your days aren't equally bad. Just like people going through life without the burden of CPTSD, you, too, will go through emotional ups and downs. Don't allow the down days to sneak up on you. By employing a couple of strategies, you can claim control of your need for emotional support.

Make it a daily habit to take a few minutes and check in with yourself. The best time of day to do this is first thing in the morning. Ask yourself what your physical, but even more importantly, your emotional needs are for the day. Do you need spiritual, emotional, or physical help and support?

- Take stock of what you're feeling right now and identify your needs. What type of support do you need?

- Do you know who to turn to in search of this support?

- Is it the support from an individual or your community that you seek?

BREAK THROUGH BARRIERS AND BOUNDARIES

Barriers and boundaries can ensure lasting relationships—as long as they're employed correctly. Let's say you build a wall around your yard. It isn't necessarily to keep people away from you but to guide visitors through the gate and where and how they need to enter your yard. If you've been building and sustaining barriers between yourself and others, it is time to break down these walls—or at least to install a gate. It is vital to let people in beyond your walls, for being stuck alone behind these barriers keeps you trapped in a lonely place where hopelessness becomes your master and your self-esteem deteriorates.

BE SPECIFIC AND ASSERTIVE IN ASKING FOR HELP

Ask for what you need in a tone that clarifies what you want. Be specific about your needs; people may want to help you but can't read your mind. So, make clear statements when you reach out to others for assistance and support.

BE GRATEFUL

When you've received the support you need, remember to be grateful. Healthy relationships thrive on mutual respect; the very least you can do to sustain the relationship is show gratitude. It is how you can be sure you'll be able to return for support when needed. If you feel emotionally able to provide support in return, do so. It will contribute to the strength of your bond and increase your sense of self-worth to make such a contribution.

ASK FOR SUPPORT AND REPEAT

Don't stop asking for support. We all need support sometimes, and you need to continue asking for what you need. So, make asking for help a regular practice in your life.

BE KIND TO YOURSELF

Self-care and being kind to yourself is also a form of support that can be hugely beneficial. Whether the trauma of your

CPTSD is only alive in your memories, or if you still find yourself trapped in such a traumatic situation, combat shame, guilt, frustration, pain, and fear with kindness to yourself and taking care of your needs.

QUICK RECAP

Sure, you can go through life solo but are the many risks, challenges, health concerns, and distress you will put yourself through worth it? When we look at history and couple it with science, it becomes clear that humans don't only need emotional support to thrive but also to survive. If you've been isolating yourself, it is time to make the necessary changes to restore these bonds. Identify the people you would like to be in contact with. Determine why and how they can contribute to your healing. Then choose to reach out and ask for help. By making different choices, you can gain a significant advance in your recovery. It is also why choices are at the heart of what we explore in our next chapter.

7

HEALING CPTSD BY MAKING DIFFERENT CHOICES

It's our intention. Our intention is everything. Nothing happens on this planet without it. Not a single thing has ever been accomplished without intention. –Jim Carrey

ALEX'S STORY

I was only 22 when I went on my first tour to Afghanistan. Thinking back on that time now, I realize that I was a mere child back then—so stupid, you know.

I remember that I was scared when I got onto the plane. Sure, there were times when I wanted to turn around. This desire was fueled every time I looked my mother in her eyes. I could see she was scared too. But then I would look at my dad and see how proud he, a veteran, was of me. Then my courage would rise again.

The day I returned, my mother begged me not to go again. She said that I did my share for my country and the people. I didn't plan to go again, but then the call came. This time around, it wasn't so scary. I'd been there, knew what it was like, and survived. This time, my mother's sadness didn't bother me as much. But this time, it was different. I went to a different base located in a very hostile area. We were under constant attack, but we kept our base protected.

Then the call came. A convoy was under attack, and we had to race in and offer support. But it was false intel, and we found ourselves trapped, but they didn't want to kill us. No, they wanted prisoners, collateral. Three of us ended up in a camp hidden away in the hills. We weren't allowed to sleep. Food was limited, and so was water. I don't want to share the details of all that happened during this time, but it was horrible. They tried to break us, and they did. No, we didn't tell them what they wanted us to say, but the day we finally broke free eight months later, we were broken—only two of us, as Bobby, didn't make it out.

It was hard to return to the US. It was a world far from where I had been for so long. It was when it all started. Even though I would sit on my parent's porch, it still felt like I was being watched, under attack, awaiting death. I might have been home, but my mind stayed in Afghanistan.

I couldn't sleep or eat, and life felt worthless. It was when the drinking started. Night after night, I would meet up with Dave who was a veteran too. He was a bit older and had been on three tours. He knew what it was like over there, and he, too, found freedom in bourbon. Night after night, we would meet up in the pub. Then it became earlier during the day.

My mother looked even worse than when I went on my tours. I couldn't look at her. I didn't want to look at her. I wanted it all to stop, my head to let go, but it wouldn't. The more I tried to forget, the worse it became. Dave and I quickly spun out of control. We fueled each other to drink more and more. We kept each other's memories alive.

Then there was that one night. Dave was in bad shape. He went to the bathroom, and when he returned, he was zoned out and pale. Before he answered what was wrong, his convulsion started. Foam came out of his mouth, and he died before my eyes.

They found a needle and pills in his pocket. I don't know what he injected. I knew it would be me next—unless I decided otherwise. I had to decide to get better.

Hell, it was hard. But I did. I did it for my parents, but also for myself. It was once I decided to get better that I could. It was when I explored how to recover and forget the crap I saw and what happened to me. It was then that I could take back control of my life. CPTSD is still part of who I am, but now I am the boss of it, and it doesn't control me anymore.

RECOVERY BEGINS BY DECIDING SO

Until the day you decide to get better, you'll remain stuck where you are. It is as simple as that: once you've made the decision, you can progress. It is also as hard as that as there is no other way, you'll gain the control you desire over your life to manage your CPTSD effectively.

I know this is no easy quest, but you must accept the past as an unchangeable part of your life and realize that while you have no control over what happened to you, you can change your future. Without making this choice, there is no hope.

Recovery, change, and choice are three undeniably linked concepts. The choice must be one made of your free will. You must have the desire to become better. Without making this choice, change will be temporary or impossible, limiting the chances of recovery.

But why does it have to be so complicated?

There are several reasons why change is so immensely hard. As we progress through these reasons, consider your life and determine which of these factors are relevant to you.

CHANGE BRINGS THE UNKNOWN

Change brings exposure to the unknown. Approaching change can be compared to approaching a dark room filled with unknowns. You can't see where you're going, what it will be like once inside the room, or even what dangers lurk in the shadows. Taking this step is difficult for anyone. It is even worse when you're already battling anxiety and panic and are constantly on the edge.

- Do the unknowns of change scare you or keep you from taking the first step toward recovery?

- What if there was nothing to fear in the room, if you just need to enter through the passage and your hand would find the light switch, waiting for you to flip it on and enjoy the freedom and serenity this room offers?

Without taking that vital step, you'll never know.

CHANGE DEMANDS PATIENCE

The mental challenges you're facing are a result of prolonged exposure to trauma. Your mind has been wounded over days, weeks, months, or even years. Now, consider how quickly it happens when you cut your finger and how long it takes for the skin to grow back and heal. Or how quickly you can break a bone in your body and how long it takes for the bone to grow back into place. The mind and the body can recover from injury. It will do so faster if it has the right support, but it still takes time.

During this time, you may experience discomfort, even pain. Your life may be disrupted, and you'll have to invest time and effort and most likely get the support of a professional. It can be so easy to jump in, all excited and motivated about the changes you need to make, but when it doesn't happen as fast as you've been hoping it would, it is easy to get despondent and give up.

- Do you have the patience and the perseverance to establish a change in your life?

- Can you be kind to yourself while your mind is slowly healing?

- If not, what is the alternative? Does this prospect hold any hope?

CHANGE REQUIRES DILIGENT ACTION

The best way to establish a significant change in your life is by taking small regular steps. These steps may seem like they don't contribute to your recovery at all, as if the effort you make daily wastes time. You may also tire of exerting yourself this way and no longer feel like you have the energy to go on.

- Do you have the diligence to stick to these steps?

- Are you open to continuously investing to reap the benefits of your efforts and a life lived well?

FEAR OF FAILURE

Are you scared you'll fail? It is okay if you are. Known symptoms of CPTSD are a lack of confidence and a lowered, may I even say crippled, self-esteem. Likely you don't consider yourself capable of taking on such a major quest as turning around your life and taking back control. There is no failure without trying, is there now? There is also no hope for improvement without taking this risk. Sometimes it is easier to weigh the positives and negatives to determine what you stand to lose if you don't try compared to what you'll lose if you fail.

- Are you scared of failure?

- What is the worst that can happen?

- Will that make your life worse than what it is now?

- But what if the worst doesn't happen and you enjoy a positive outcome? Isn't it worth at least trying to establish a change in your life?

HOW TO MAKE THE CHOICE TO HEAL

Once you've made the very important decision to heal and set your intentions on recovery, you've taken the first step, and the hardest part of the process from here onwards is to remain diligent in taking small steps all the way. While you might have made the big initial decision to step onto the road of recovery, one of the steps you'll have to take daily is to make that choice again and again. Yes, recovery demands the daily decision to do what is necessary to better your life and to have a more positive impact on those you love.

RESEARCH RESOURCES

Now, let's move on to explore a couple of helpful tips. It is time to get proactive and research all the available options you have access to that will support you on your journey. I've already urged you to follow a combined effort by including prescription medication and therapy treatment in your recovery plan. Now, you need to explore what resources you have access to in your area.

FINDING YOUR THERAPIST

Seeing a therapist for the first time may feel daunting. This is especially true when you've been planning to see a professional for a while. That said, it remains essential that you choose the right therapist for your CPTSD and your personality. It must be someone with whom you feel comfortable sharing your inner secrets and stories, and someone you can build a rapport with.

I urge you to see a couple of therapists to determine who is the best fit for you. Ask the professional all the questions you need answers to during your first session. Consider questions like the following:

- What qualifications do you have?
- How long have you been in this specific field?
- How much of your focus has been on CPTSD?
- How do your treatment sessions work?
- What is your emergency policy?
- How will you determine my progress?
- What treatment do you recommend in my case?
- How long will it be before I start to feel a difference?
- How much do you charge?

THE COST FACTOR

Yes, the price may bring an abrupt end to your plans. The reality is that therapist fees can be somewhat expensive as you're paying for specialized care. Know that when you're calling on a mental health professional, they have been investing time and money into their career to help people like yourself effectively. It is this level of expertise that you're paying for.

- Do you have medical insurance that is willing to pay for this expense?

- Are there any mental health services offered free of charge in your area? Perhaps at a community clinic?

Remember that it isn't only your treatment that will come with a price tag, since you'll also have to pay for your prescription meds. But if you have medical insurance, you'll find they are often keen on footing the bills to give you the support you need.

However, if none of these seem to be a possibility to you and you need to settle your bills yourself, it doesn't have to be the end of your journey, and you don't have to remain trapped for the rest of your life. No, where there is a will, there is a way, and I know deep down you have a strong desire to get better for yourself and your loved ones.

- So, consider the goodwill of others. Do you have someone who might be willing and able to assist you financially?

- Have you considered alternative ways of gathering funds to settle this bill?

Crowdfunding may be a last resort too. Consider getting a campaign running to source the financial aid you need.

KNOW YOUR WHY

Change isn't easy, but it is possible, and it becomes easier when you know why you're doing it. Knowing your *why—*

even listing the many reasons why you're putting yourself through the process of change and placing it where you can see it regularly—will help keep you motivated when your excitement and inspiration are low.

It is also important to remember that humans tend to exert themselves much more to avoid the things we don't want to have as part of our lives than to get what we desire. So, when you list your *whys*, place enough emphasis on what you want to avoid in your life. Let's take the example of someone who is grossly overweight to explain what I mean. Let's call our person Doug. Doug has been overweight his entire life, and while he wanted to lose weight and even went on diets a couple of times, he just gave up easily. Sure, he wants to look toned and attractive, but that just doesn't seem to be enough motivation to steer clear from takeout and to spend time in the gym.

One day, Doug started to feel awful at work, he collapsed, and the paramedics came to fetch him. Doug had a heart attack, but he survived. His doctor gave him a stern warning, "Doug if you're not going to lose forty pounds over the next couple of months, you'll most likely not see the end of next year."

Doug's children are still young, he wants to see them grow up and fears being unable to do that if he doesn't bring about change. He would hate to have his kids grow up without a dad just because he didn't do what he had to stay healthy. Even the idea of his wife remarrying after he died and having his kids call someone else Dad freaks him out. As Doug's future looks bleak and he wants to avoid the worst outcome at all costs, he takes his weight loss seriously and remains committed to a healthy lifestyle—a choice that saves his life.

What Doug wanted—being toned and attractive wasn't sufficient inspiration. What Doug wanted to avoid inspired and motivated him to keep up his new healthy habits.

- What does your future look like if you don't choose recovery and healing?

- Who will get hurt by your failure to take care of yourself?

- What experiences will you miss out on if you don't decide to take control of your life?

- How much longer do you want to simmer in misery over the past you can't change and waste your future too?

- List your *whys* and place this list where you can see it often and remind yourself regularly what the price to pay would be if you don't persevere.

ACCEPT THE PAST

This brings me to accepting what you can't change. Return to the Serenity prayer and read every word to be sure you grasp what it means exactly. You don't have to be religious to make this prayer your motto, as this is also expressing your desire to accept, out loud, a step to manifest the life you want.

I want to share another image with you. Animals in captivity are controversial, and stories covering this concern often make headlines. At times, these articles center around elephants in captivity, whether to perform in the circus or be used as a tourist attraction or as working animals. Therefore, it is not an unfamiliar image to visualize when I ask you to think about a captured elephant tied down with a chain around its leg. This chain keeps the animal trapped, but in reality, the elephant is strong enough to break this chain. The problem the elephant is facing is that it doesn't realize it has the power to break free. It has been held down in this manner for so long and is surrounded by other elephants kept in the same manner. It doesn't realize its strength. So, it is, in fact, the animal's belief that it is too weak to break free that keeps it trapped and not so much the chain itself.

- Are you an elephant, believing that your past is keeping you trapped?
- Do you realize that you have the power to break free from this chain?

It is time to reclaim your power and live at full capacity, but this will remain an impossible quest for as long as you hold onto the past. I know it is hard, but it is possible to set yourself free.

QUICK RECAP

Nothing in life happens until we decide to make it happen. In the next couple of chapters, I share several more helpful strategies you can employ to break free from the past, unlock your future, and remain in control of your life, but it all starts with one step, choosing to get better.

What do you need to make that decision? Do you have to be confronted with the death of another like Alex in our story? Do you need to have a near-death experience yourself? Do you have to lose loved ones first as relationships crumble? I'm encouraging you to wait no more. Life is for the living; make the most of yours and break free from the past. You're not responsible for what has happened, nor are you guilty of anything, as past events were beyond your control, but you are in charge of your today and many tomorrows. Choose change today—break free and live. You can learn more about one of these steps in the next chapter.

8

HEALING CPTSD USING EXPOSURE THERAPY

We are more often frightened than hurt; and we suffer more from imagination than from reality. –Seneca

So far, I've been highlighting the immense impact that past traumatic events have on your mind and body, and now I throw this quote by Seneca at you. Does it sound like I am saying never underestimate the impact the series of traumatic events you endured have on you, but also never overestimate it either? I understand if you wonder whose side I am on, but let me explain, and soon it will become clear how this approach can bring about the improvement you desire.

Earlier on, we explored how the brain processes trauma. One of the concerns we touched on was that the brain tends to build more trauma on top of existing trauma. Remember how I explained that an entire crowd could witness a traumatic event and all have different perspectives of what happened and how it impacted them? The more time that passes between the actual event and the recollection of the event, the more traumatic these experiences tend to become as the brain is wired to color these moments in. By no means does it diminish the severity of the events from which you stepped away as a survivor, but it highlights the fact that you need to confront memories to determine the truth so that you can unburden yourself of those bits the brain has added and only deal with the factual events.

This is one of the breakthroughs you'll attain from exposure therapy. But what is exposure therapy?

AN OVERVIEW OF EXPOSURE THERAPY

Exposure therapy is a technique specifically created to help people confront their fears with facts, providing the support they need to overcome anxiety and break free from the grip of fear and avoidance.

The word avoidance becomes relevant here, with avoidance being one of the three classic behavioral symptoms of CPTSD. It is coupled with re-experiencing symptoms and arousal. Avoidance is the classic approach to keep your life from spinning out of control for the time being, as you procrastinate on the choice to get better.

Re-experiencing takes on many forms and can occur anytime, day or night. While your dreams are often riddled with nightmares, keeping you trapped in the same traumatic events you couldn't escape from for so long, you can also experience flashbacks while awake.

Once you re-experience these events, there is an immediate arousal. The SNS jumps to activate the stress response, alerting your body. This arousal occurs mentally and physiologically, as we've already discussed. In short, it is a highly unpleasant state to be in.

Gradually, you become aware of what serves as triggers bringing these memories to the surface, and that is when avoidance kicks in. You may avoid certain places, events, situations, or people as exposure to any of these tends to take you right back to when you were trapped within the trauma. Now, as your brain is building on top of the existing trauma, it often happens that you gradually begin to avoid even aspects of life that don't serve as triggers for reliving the trauma, but in fact, triggers reliving the traumatic state you've experienced during your flashbacks. So, the list of things you want to avoid grows longer, and eventually, you live your entire life in isolation. This is, of course, as discussed, another grave concern that causes your CPTSD to worsen.

Through exposure therapy, you can remove the sting from what is hurting you so deeply and set yourself free to live your life without having to avoid many of its aspects. For example, let's say you have a phobia for enclosed spaces. It means you need to get into an elevator to get to your office on the 16th floor of the building daily. Each time your anxiety levels spike, placing your body and mind in a high-risk state. In exposure therapy, your therapist will work with you to gradually increase exposure to what you fear so deeply so that you can become familiar with it, and then it is no longer so scary. The more you have this controlled exposure, the easier it becomes to expose yourself to these matters, and the greater your freedom becomes.

CAROL'S STORY

Carol's entire life changed when she was 15 years old. Until that point in her life, she lived the carefree life of being an only child. She grew up in a prominent suburb with large houses and long driveways. She had many friends in her neighborhood, and all the kids in the area had similar lives—there was no lack of money, and they enjoyed immense freedom. Her dad was a reputable plastic surgeon, and her mom was a socialite.

One afternoon after school, Carol was walking with her friends to the mall when a van suddenly pulled up next to them and grabbed her. She was kidnapped for about five days until negotiations were finalized between her dad, his attorneys, the authorities, and her kidnappers. She was freed from captivity but never from what had happened to her.

Carol suffered from CPTSD. Every time she set foot on the street, her mind would be bombarded with fear, she would be on high alert, and panic would kick in when there was any sudden movement or noise close to her. It became too much for her, and the teenager became homebound as she desperately wanted to avoid the street. Carol didn't understand that it wasn't the street that posed a danger, it was the kidnappers, and she could and should step out on the streets again to live a healthy and balanced life.

As the situation got out of control, her parents convinced her of the need to get proper therapy, and that is how she ended up in exposure therapy. During her first sessions, her therapist worked hard to gain Carol's trust. Gradually, the rapport expanded between them. It was evident what Carol had to do. She had to face her fear—getting back on the street again.

It was a lengthy process, but Carol realized that the more time she spent on the street under complete supervision, the easier it became to walk out in public again. This was because her last impression of the street was linked to such a traumatic event that she couldn't get past it. It was only once she forced herself to face what she had been avoiding all this time that she could form new memories and make healthy connections with living a normal life.

To call facing your fears the foundation of exposure therapy might be a very basic comparison, but it is indeed what it means.

As this means that you may enter a high-risk situation and will need emotional support, I recommend that you settle for this type of therapy under the guidance of a mental health professional. But there are certain steps you too can take to practice this on your own time.

THINGS TO KNOW BEFORE OPTING FOR EXPOSURE THERAPY

Opting for exposure therapy may leave you feeling scared. That is okay, as being scared will make you aware of the steps you need to take to ensure your mental and physical wellness is protected during exposure. Yet, when you follow the next strategies, you'll be perfectly safe and will be able to enjoy the benefits of this kind of therapy.

HAVE EMOTIONAL SUPPORT ON HAND

When you are using exposure therapy with the help of a mental health professional, you have someone with you to help you through these moments of elevated anxiety. If you opt for exposure therapy at home, this will not be the case. So, before venturing any further, identify who will be your support network when you opt for doing this type of therapy at home. Be sure to have someone who can help to calm you down and work through your anxiety.

RESEARCH ANXIETY

Learn as much as possible about anxiety and how it impacts your body and mind. Understanding what is happening in your body removes a large part of the hold that anxiety has on you. Understanding what happens in your body will remove fears that may surface during such an attack. For many, having an anxiety attack often feels like they are dying. This feeling will increase your anxiety levels and push it out of control. However, it becomes far less scary once you understand what is causing your heart to race during these moments and that it is a perfectly normal physiological response. So, learn as much as possible to prepare yourself physically and mentally. Once armed with knowledge, anxiety becomes a far lesser concern.

LIST TIPS TO REDUCE YOUR ANXIETY INSTANTLY

Let me expand on the previous point by saying it will be helpful to draft a list of possible steps to reduce your anxiety quickly. At that moment, when anxiety levels peak, it may feel unbearable. You may not think clearly. It is why it is so important that you compile a list of actionable steps you can take without thinking about it to alleviate your state. Be sure to inform your support person of what to do, too, so that their support can be helpful to you.

TIPS TO REDUCE ANXIETY QUICKLY

Tips you can add to this list would be breathing exercises. Inhale slowly and deliberately, focusing on how the air passes through your airways, which will take your focus off your anxiety and trigger the PSNS to restore a sense of greater calm.

Another approach is the 3-3-3 rule. In this grounding exercise, where you have to shift your focus to your surroundings, search for three things you see and three sounds you hear, and then move three body parts.

TAKE SMALL STEPS

The key to successful exposure therapy is to avoid the deep end. Don't overwhelm yourself at the start. This is not the kind of situation where you can just rip off the band aid and get it over and done with, and don't allow anyone else to convince you otherwise. Remember, you are taking control of your life; the first step would be to take control of your recovery. Opt for gradual exposure to aspects that resemble what you fear and what usually serves as a trigger.

For example, reverting to the fear of getting into an elevator. Start by going to the elevator and pressing the button, but don't get in. Simply stand there; all you need to do is to press the button. A word of advice is to choose an elevator carrying less traffic as you don't want to upset others, taking out their frustration or irritation on you for slowing them down. Next, you can get into the elevator, but let your support person hold the door so you know the doors won't close behind you. Just get used to being in this space. Once you feel okay with a certain step, you can push yourself to do something slightly more intense. Keep this up until you don't feel anxious anymore.

Remember that once the anxiety linked to a certain object, situation, or event is removed, there will be no more triggers to avoid.

IDENTIFY YOUR FEELINGS

While exposing yourself to your fears gradually, become aware of your feelings. Anxiety and fear may overshadow your other emotions, but they aren't all you feel during these moments. Determine what feelings surface and identify them. List them, explore them, link these feelings to other occasions, and determine their origins. Next, you can combat these feelings by determining whether they are relevant. Your progress will gain even greater momentum once you've busted these feelings as unnecessary additions to your situation.

TAKE BREAKS WHEN NECESSARY

If it all becomes too much, it is fine to take a step back for a few days but return later. Sometimes you may even notice that you've improved in the absence of exposure. This can be that you've given your brain time to process this new experience, helping it to heal.

RELY ON ACCOUNTABILITY

Your support person can fulfill a dual role in your recovery. While this person can be there to give you the support you need and help restore a sense of calm during an anxiety attack, they can also be the one you ask to keep you accountable to maintain the process. Accountability is one of the tips to ensure progress during change. It can be easy to flake on yourself when taking all of this on as a solo exercise, but it is much harder to avoid doing what is necessary when someone else is keeping you accountable.

Once you start facing your fears, you can distinguish between your actual trauma and what your brain has added to your memories. Once you've scraped off all the layers your trauma has accumulated, you'll be better equipped to work through the actual trauma similarly.

QUESTIONS TO ASK WHEN SEEKING AN EXPOSURE THERAPIST

The alternative is to work with a professional to help you face your fears in a secure environment. You can use the following pointers as discussion points during your first session to determine whether you've found the best mental health professional to address your needs.

- Determine how many patients like you they helped in the past.

- How good is their understanding of CPTSD—they should know the difference between trauma, PTSD, and CPTSD.

- Find out how they ensure you remain in a safe environment.

- Determine their fees.

- Find out if they offer after-hour care when you experience a panic emergency.

QUICK RECAP

Through familiarity, scary things can lose the power they have over you. But if you avoid facing your fears, your brain will continuously make them worse than they truly are. Exposure therapy is a trusted type of treatment to shed your fears and free your life from triggers that will cause a physiological response, keeping you trapped.

While it is important to face your fears, it is also necessary that you become familiar with what you're feeling. You can find peace and gain control by identifying your feelings and sharing what is happening in your inner world—more on how to achieve this in our next chapter.

9

HEALING CPTSD BY COMMUNICATING YOUR INNER WORLD

We're often afraid of being vulnerable, but vulnerability creates genuine connection. –Gabby Bernstein

It can be hard to share your emotions for several reasons. You can be scared that by doing so, you make yourself vulnerable to others. As you've already been a trauma victim, the mere idea of being so vulnerable again is far too much to ask. It can be that talking about your emotions is too painful, so you prefer to box them up inside. Or perhaps your trauma so brutally damaged your self-worth that you lack the confidence to share your story and feel that nobody will listen to you.

- What is your reason for bottling up your trauma and the emotions disturbing your inner peace?

- Is it the case that you may not have anyone you can confide in?

If the latter is the case, I urge you to search for a reputable dialectical behavior therapist near you. Dialectical behavior therapy (DBT) is a type of talk therapy, a treatment option designed to help clients manage emotions better and overcome mental challenges. Initially, it was developed to aid those battling borderline personality disorder as it is heavily focused on ensuring more effective emotional management and forming strong and healthy bonds. Today, DBT is a trusted therapy treatment to address depression, suicidal notions, trauma, anxiety, eating disorders, and more mental health concerns.

If you choose this option, your therapist will guide you through strategies to communicate your inner world. But DBT isn't the only way to improve your mental and physical health by sharing your feelings and what is happening inside your mind.

MEL'S STORY

Mel's family was extremely poor. She is the only child of a single mother, and the two of them moved in with her grandmother when her father walked out on them. Her grandma refers to their family's hardships as a generational curse. But Mel always thought it was the wrongdoings of the current generation and not so much ancestral wrongdoings that caused her family all the pain and suffering they were going through. This mindset was only further confirmed when her mother got a new boyfriend, Felix. She couldn't stand the way the man looked at her, a girl of only 10 years old. Her situation got far worse when her mother came home one day, telling her to pack her bags because the two of them were going to live with Felix. He got a contract in another city, and they will build a life with him there.

Mel remembers all her tears because she didn't want to leave her grandmother's house. She remembers arriving in a new city, not knowing anyone nor having anything familiar with her surroundings. And then she also remembers how Felix came into her room the first night after moving in, what he told her to do to him, what he did to her, and how awful it made her feel. He threatened to throw her and her mother out on the streets if she dared say anything to anyone. She was trapped, and night after night, he would come into her room, do the same things, smell the same way, and hurt her badly. At first, it was just touching and kissing, but after a couple of weeks, he raped her—every night for more than a year.

A broken child showed up on her grandmother's door one day. Once courage and opportunity met, Mel took her chance and ran away. She wouldn't talk to her grandma or say anything about what happened. However, her grandmother took her to the community clinic, where she got medical care, and her abuse was confirmed. Still, Mel didn't say a thing. She was trapped in her head. She would cry in her sleep at night, and during the daytime, she would stay indoors.

Her grandmother was patient. She didn't force her to talk, but she assured the child that she was there to listen when she was ready to speak. After five months, Mel finally dared to share what had happened.

"Once I could find my voice to share how I felt, things started to change for me. I became lighter inside—my burden wasn't so heavy anymore. I took almost two years to step outside, trust people again, and regain control over my life. I had to deal with what happened and change my perspective on my past. Through many conversations with my grandmother, I could see my father, who left, my mother, who never protected me, and Felix—the monster in my nightmares, in a different light. Not one in which what they did was right in any way, but one that allowed me to forgive them so that I could be free," Mel shares her story.

It has been a decade since Mel's escape. Today, she is working as a nurse at a different clinic. She married a kind and understanding man and had two young kids. She also has a room in her home for her grandmother, the one person she could talk to and whose willing and caring ears could help Mel find healing.

WHY YOU MUST SHARE YOUR TRAUMA

You'll be surprised to learn how many people are willing to listen when you're ready to talk. These people want to help you and build a bond with you but can't do so as long as they don't know what you went through.

TO HELP PEOPLE UNDERSTAND

People won't understand your trauma unless you share it with them. You need to be open and honest and let others know how you feel, why you feel this way, why you have certain triggers, behave in a certain manner, or struggle to deal with certain everyday-life events. Mel later on shared in her story that when she initially met her husband, he didn't know what happened to her.

"At first, I liked him but didn't feel worthy of his attention. The more he tried to get my interest, the more I thought there was no way someone like him would be interested in me. I was damaged goods. But gradually, he gained my trust, and we became friends.

Yet, even when we were friends, we would go somewhere, and something would trigger me. For example, I would see someone that looked like Felix, and that would set off my anxiety, and my behavior would become completely erratic. I would leave him in the middle of a restaurant or a park and run as fast as possible.

One day, he caught up with me, and I broke down. I almost screamed at him and told him why I wasn't good enough to be in his company. I expected that he would walk away—run if he was me—but he didn't. He sat beside me, put his arm around my shoulders, and said he was sorry I had to endure so much. It was when I realized that I had to be honest with him and share my story. He was the first person, except for my gran, whom I told about what happened. Since then, I've become more comfortable sharing my trauma, which has helped me form strong bonds with people who became my support network. These are the people who help me to manage my CPTSD so that I can enjoy a happy and balanced life."

TO HELP OTHERS TO SUPPORT YOU

It is only once those around you understand the emotions, thoughts, and triggers you're battling, that they can effectively begin to help you. Sometimes all you need is just support, or an ear willing to listen, but you won't have that if people don't know what you're going through.

TO STRENGTHEN YOUR BONDS

If your behavior is erratic toward people who have no idea what challenges you're facing, it will likely put unnecessary strain on your relationship. But once others know what your challenges are and how they can support you, the bond will grow stronger and you'll have the support network you need.

HOW TO SHARE YOUR TRAUMA

This can be a hard conversation; understandably, it isn't something you would like to share with a loved one or friend over coffee. But it is also best not to work yourself up too much about having this conversation, as this may make it even harder to say what you feel.

START BY SHARING YOUR TRIGGERS

Triggers may be a more effective manner to ease into these conversations. Explain what the triggers are that are causing you to say or do things that seem out of the norm. If you've been spending quite a bit of time with someone you care about, it is likely they've already seen something unusual in your behavior, and it will only help your bond when you explain why that is.

By sharing your triggers, you also provide the other person with the necessary understanding of how they can support you effectively and help you live your desired life.

SHARE WHAT YOU FEEL COMFORTABLE WITH

While I encourage you to share your trauma with those close to you, it remains up to you how much or little you're willing to share with a specific person or at a certain time in your relationship. For example, you may be ready to admit that you've been exposed to a series of traumatic events, but you may not be ready to share the details of what happened to you, and that is fine.

There are two people in the relationship, and both should feel comfortable with the conversation. It can also be that sharing too much detail at once can be daunting for the other person to process. It can lead them to behave in a way they may regret later. So, let the information stream flow at a pace you're comfortable with sharing and the other person is comfortable with hearing.

KNOW THERE WILL BE QUESTIONS

When you share information about your trauma, you can be sure the other person will have questions about what you tell them. These questions mostly originate from their need to gain a deeper understanding of what happened so that they can provide you with better support.

While you should know that these questions will come, know that you don't have to answer all these questions at once. You can even say that you know there are questions but that you would like to address these at a later stage. If the other person has shared some of their questions, you can think about how you can best answer them when the moment presents itself.

UNDERSTAND THAT YOUR TRAUMA WILL CAUSE AN EMOTIONAL RESPONSE

Humans tend to be empathic, so when hearing your story of heartache, pain, and the immense trauma you've been through, it is a normal response if the other person shows emotional distress. Reassure them that having questions and expressing their emotions is okay.

CALL A TIME-OUT IF NEEDED

You can also call a time-out if you're no longer comfortable with the situation, sharing your story, or the response you're getting from the other person. Remember, you're in control of your journey toward recovery, and you take control of how much you share, when, and with whom.

But what do you do if you've shared all your most intimate secrets and it still appears the other person doesn't understand? Was that a mistake, then?

No, soon, we'll explore the many benefits you can gain from sharing your trauma so it is never a mistake.

If so, you can expand on how the trauma affected your life. Trauma doesn't affect everyone in the same manner, and how it impacts your life may be entirely different from how the other person would expect trauma to affect their life. It is not always easy to grasp how trauma can affect your mental and physical state, and this is even more true if the other person has never been exposed to trauma themselves.

Are you still struggling to convey your inner landscape in a way the other person understands? Try the following tips:

- Choose the right place to continue with the conversation where you can talk without being overheard or disturbed. Seek a spot where you and the other person can show your emotions without being observed by others who are not part of the conversation. These conversations often bring about tears, and many people may feel uncomfortable crying where others can see them.

- Find the right moment to bring up the conversation again. Ensure you can have this conversation undisturbed and without any time restrictions. It may be a longer conversation than you initially anticipated, and there might be much emotional discharge that would need to occur before you can continue with your day.

- Don't use words that are hard to understand. Rather share your trauma in your words and use personal terms you're comfortable using.

- Share your inner landscape by naming your feelings. The other person may never know what exactly you've been through, but if you state that you felt humiliated, hurt, sad, rejected, or any other emotions, they can identify with what you say. Most people have a relatively wide emotional repertoire, so while they can never understand how trauma exposure made you feel, they can determine how it would've made them feel.

- Say what you need. You're sharing this sensitive information with another for two reasons. You want them to understand you, your words, and your behavior better. But you also want them to support you in your healing. What do you want from them? It may be merely understanding you're seeking, or perhaps it is more that you're looking for support. Either way, express what you want to allow the other person to decide whether they can give you what you need.

QUICK RECAP

Shared heartache is halved heartache. Whenever you talk about the traumatic events you've been exposed to, you create another opportunity to work through the distress and emotional pain you've been exposed to. It is how you gradually process the situation until nothing is left to process.

By sharing what has happened to you, you enable the other person to understand and support you more effectively. It is how you can strengthen your bonds with your loved ones and gradually expand your support network.

During these conversations, you need to express how the trauma has affected your life and what negative emotions it stirs in you. It is one way to shed yourself from these negative emotions. In the next chapter, we explore more ways to free yourself from these emotions.

10

HEALING CPTSD BY DEALING WITH NEGATIVE EMOTIONS

When embraced and accepted, negative emotions can be a powerful catalyst to positive change in one's life and can lead to deeper feeling of meaning and authenticity. –Paul TP Wong

Nature is crippled when the state of balance and harmony trips too far to a specific side. Even the life cycle centers around birth and death; together, harmony exists. We can't have good in our lives without bad.

And in the same manner, we can't have only positive emotions without experiencing negative ones. After exposure to a series of traumatic events, you may feel burdened with negative emotions but don't ignore these feelings or wish them away, for they, too, have a role to fulfill in your life.

JENNY'S STORY

Jenny and Clyde got married on a beautiful autumn day. Her mother warned her not to get married during a season synonymous with death as it is an omen not serving any married couple well. Jenny laughed at her superstition as she saw the beauty of dancing leaves in gold, copper, caramel, and orange tones.

The next year, when autumn changed the colors of the leaves, Jenny knew her mother's words had come true. On their honeymoon, Clyde's abusive side had already reared its head. He would get angry at her over the silliest things, and when he was so livid, he would scream at her right in public. The first time it happened, she burst into tears, causing quite a scene. A man approached Clyde, resulting in a serious altercation and adding to her humiliation. So, Jenny quickly learned not to go against Clyde.

She hoped it would improve when they returned home, but it only got worse. Clyde would get furious if the food didn't have enough salt to his taste. She screamed back at him one night, and he punched her right in the eye. The next morning her eye was blue and swollen shut, and she had to call in sick for a week.

A few weeks later, he split open her lip with his palm, and she called in sick again. But it was when she called in sick for the fifth time in six months, as her ribs were too bruised for her to even walk upright, her manager told her she was fired. She was relieved that there was one place she didn't have to lie to about what was happening in her marriage, but now she was also left without an income and completely dependent on Clyde.

The night she told him that she got fired was the worst. She thought he would never stop as his hands rained punishment on her already bruised and battered body. Jenny became withdrawn. She was too ashamed to set foot outside their home. Clyde forced her to break contact with her family, but this was a brittle bond already. He would go off to work daily, laughing, making friends, and being his charming self, and at night, she would have to hear what a pathetic person she was. Then, he didn't come home every night anymore. When he did, he smelled like perfume, and she knew he had replaced her, but that didn't upset her. No, it relieved her as now his attention was distracted, and maybe he would leave her alone.

Why did she stay? Well, one day she got into the car to leave, and for some reason, as she pulled out of the garage, he pulled in right behind her. He scolded her severely, asking her who was supposed to take up her job if she left. He hit her, and as she fell, she bumped her head. She woke up on the couch when it was dark outside. She was all alone that night, vomiting due to a serious concussion. He took her phone and locked her in. She was trapped and stayed that way for far too long.

Four years and 56 days after they said their vows, the police knocked on the front door. Clyde hadn't been home for three days. Jenny was in bed with a broken rib and one eye still swollen shut. Somebody broke down the front door. Clyde had been in an accident. He passed away. Instead of finding a grieving widow, they found Jenny, a woman with a broken mind and body. But finally, she was free.

"The days after they came to tell me Clyde died, my body was too broken to think or feel anything, but as I gradually got physically stronger, my mind began to wonder, and all the things Clyde said and did to me seemed to surface. I was humiliated over how they found me and embarrassed every time someone asked me why I put up with this for so long. I began to feel like it was my fault. I saw photos of Clyde's memorial service. There were so many people crying over their loss. Why did so many people miss him, except me? I blamed myself. I think many other people did too.

At times, guilt, shame, humiliation, embarrassment, disgrace, anger, fear, and anxiety pressed me to the floor. These negative emotions became too much. I couldn't breathe, sleep, or eat. It took me so long to get the help I needed. I felt so alone, but whenever anyone reached out to me, I pushed them away. It didn't feel like I deserved to be helped. I didn't want to talk about what happened. No, I didn't even want to think about it, yet it was all I could think about. When I was discharged, I returned home. It was the only place I knew. It was strange, though. Clyde was there even though he wasn't.

I couldn't sleep at night and started to dig into his whisky. It felt brave…and it helped me to sleep. So, I did it again and again. Fortunately, Clyde didn't have a will, and being his wife, I got, by default, all he had. It was more than I expected or was used to, but it didn't matter as I drank more, and whisky was all that mattered.

My mother, of all people, came to fetch me. She took me home, sat me down, and got me help. Recovery was a long journey, but I made it. I survived. I learned." Jenny's story is in many ways quite unique but also so similar to the story of many trauma survivors.

NEGATIVE EMOTIONS ARE NORMAL TO FEEL

When you bump your toe, it is sore. When you cut your finger, it bleeds. The same principle is valid; you will feel negative emotions when exposed to trauma. These emotions can be sadness or anger, humiliation or fear, or any of the emotions in between. Hiding the pain in your toe or the bleeding finger won't solve the problem. It won't bring you any relief. So, why would hiding your emotions bring you relief?

Let's continue with the toe and finger analogy. By bumping your toe, you learn to be more careful when walking barefoot. In the future, you may switch on the light if an accident occurs when you enter a dark room. When cutting your finger, you may learn to improve your knife skills or that knife accidents are more prone to happen with a blunt knife than a sharp one, and next time you'll sharpen the knife first before cutting anything. It will surely not be the last time that any of these accidents happen, but every time it does happen, your knowledge base expands, and your skills to avoid these incidents increase and improve.

Similarly, experiencing negative emotions also teaches us more about ourselves. You gain greater insights into what you like and dislike, how you want to be treated by others, and what type of treatment repels you as it is so disrespectful or hurtful toward you. While it is never a pleasant experience to be flushed with negative emotions, it is a necessary experience to get to know yourself, what you're capable of, and how resilient you truly are in the face of adversity.

WHY YOU SHOULDN'T SUPPRESS YOUR EMOTIONS

There is a widespread myth about suppressing your emotions. It is the belief that the more you suppress your emotions, the quicker they'll fade. This is the worst advice you'll ever receive regarding your emotions. In reality, it is quite the opposite. Numerous studies show that the more you suppress your emotions, the stronger they become (Pisano, n.d.).

Furthermore, these studies also conclude that when you suppress your emotions, you're putting yourself at risk of mental and physical reactions. I am referring here to concerns like depression and anxiety and mental health concerns that harm your physical health, too (Pisano, n.d.).

One more insight gained from these study results is that emotional suppression triggers the Vagus nerve to place the body in the stress response for long periods, which can be detrimental to your health.

What is the alternative, then? Apply effective emotional management. We can break this process down into a few smaller steps. Acknowledge that these emotions exist, accept them as yours, and confront them to determine whether they are true or relevant to the situation. But let's make this more practical.

HEALTHY WAYS TO REGULATE YOUR EMOTIONS

The following steps are all part of a process you can use to claim your emotions, positive and negative, and employ them to achieve the self-development you need to reclaim control over your life in the presence of CPTSD.

STEP #1: IDENTIFY YOUR FEELINGS

Take a moment to reach a state of greater self-awareness. You can achieve this by finding a space where you can sit undisturbed for a few minutes. Take a few deep breaths to calm your body and your mind. Shift your focus to your inner landscape.

What are the feelings you feel? Is it perhaps anxiety, fear, guilt, shame, anger, or resentment?

List the feelings as you identify them. Remember that several emotions can surface at a time, and sometimes these feelings come and go, so spend enough time to see what is happening on the feelings front.

STEP #2: DETERMINE WHEN YOU FEEL THESE FEELINGS

Once you've identified and listed the feelings you experience, it becomes easier to determine when you feel them during the day. By keeping a daily journal, capturing the events of your day, you create a record of your feelings and how you respond. This journal will also show you certain patterns, making it easier to identify times, locations, events, situations, or people that serve as triggers causing these emotions to surface.

STEP #3: IDENTIFY YOUR THOUGHTS LINKED TO THESE FEELINGS

It is not always outside factors that serve as triggers for an emotional response. Often, this can be internal conditions too. While a journal will help capture the events of your day, you must employ greater awareness to determine your thoughts when a certain emotion becomes problematic. You may have to make notes as it happens to capture these thoughts to establish a pattern or link between your thoughts and emotions.

STEP #4: TRACK YOUR RECOVERY

One more thing you can keep track of in your journal is your recovery. Why is this important? I assume you've already chosen to heal and employed several of the steps presented thus far. I've mentioned how hard it can be to persevere in taking small steps, but it is also important to maintain continuous action. Noticing your progress can serve as additional encouragement, confirming you're moving forward on this journey. So, if your day was great, jot it down. But also state what made it so great for these are the factors you want to expand on in your life.

STEP #5: LEARN FROM YOUR EMOTIONS

Every emotion you experience holds the power to teach you something. But these lessons can get easily lost if you do not remember them. So, when you find a certain emotion that appears quite often, ask yourself what you can learn from it. Once you've determined the lesson the emotions want to teach you, it will fade naturally.

Use these steps as your foundation; from here onwards, effective emotional management will become much easier to maintain.

QUICK RECAP

So, now you know that it is natural to experience positive and negative emotions. We've touched on the necessity of experiencing emotions from both sides of the spectrum to enjoy a fulfilled and balanced life. Suppressing your emotions constitutes bad emotional management, and a healthier approach would be to acknowledge, accept, and confront your emotions. Through emotional management, you can create a peaceful internal space. In the next chapter, we'll expand on this and determine how you can ensure you also find yourself in safe external spaces to flourish, live your desired life, and be happy.

11

HEALING CPTSD BY CREATING SAFE SPACES

The world can only seem a safe place when we feel safe inside. –Agapi Stassinopoulos

Children are born into the world daily. In many families, this is a moment of huge celebration. The child has parents who love it and want the best for their baby. They nurture the child, protect it, and create a physically and mentally safe environment for it to grow and develop. But this isn't the case for all babies. Sadly, many babies born daily enter a world ridden with violence, fear, and a shortage of necessities like food, clean water, and health care.

CHIDI'S STORY

Chidi's dad was killed in guerrilla warfare a few weeks before his birth. His mother's heart was broken over the loss of her husband. So, when Chidi was born, she was emotionally and physically depleted. The birth had complications, and while Chidi survived, his mother didn't. The young boy was left an orphan in a village impoverished by persistent warfare. It was a place with limited infrastructure, no formal health care, limited food, and education. Boys were trained by their fathers to fight early on to protect what was theirs. Girls had to stay at home to learn from their mothers.

The young boy was taken in by an old lady in the village. She had already lost all her sons and her husband in the persistent fighting, and as she was alone, she saw the boy and decided to give him a home. Nobody else wanted to take on this burden. While the old woman could give him a roof and love, she couldn't give him everything. There were days when there was no food to eat, and she couldn't provide him with a safe space to stay. When the guerrilla fighters came into his village, Chidi was five and hiding behind a heap of firewood. He saw how they shot several people in the village's dusty streets and set houses on fire. That was when Chidi's image of the world began to take a negative turn.

When Chidi was 12, he woke up one morning; he was surprised that the woman, the only mother he had ever known, wasn't awake yet. He tried to wake her up, and her body was stiff and cold. The only person who ever cared for him was gone from his life. He stayed in the village. Every day was a battle to find food, ensure his protection, and stay alive.

He was 15 when a missionary came to visit the troubled area. He met Chidi and, considering his circumstances, offered to take the boy with him when he returned home to America. Chidi agreed. He thought he could escape this hardship, the horror, violence, death, and being in a constant state of fear. But while he could leave the environment, he was so familiar with, the environment didn't leave him, as his memories stuck with him even when he was thousands of miles away from where he was born. Chidi was in a safe physical environment, and while that was helpful, what he needed to help him let go of the past, a life riddled with one traumatic experience after another, was psychological safety.

So, when Chidi realized he was in a safe space and surrounded by people who cared about him, his mind and body's healing could begin.

WHAT IS PSYCHOLOGICAL SAFETY?

Psychological safety is built on the foundation that you can speak your mind, express your beliefs and feelings, and ask questions without fearing negative consequences. The definition implies, by default, that you are part of a larger body of people or a team. This team can also be a family, a group of friends, coworkers, a support network, or even on a wider scale, your community.

Psychological safety is established when there is trust, inclusion, safety, and the freedom to challenge existing mindsets without being marginalized, humiliated, reprimanded, or punished for your beliefs.

THE BENEFITS WHEN YOU FIND YOURSELF IN A SAFE SPACE

While it is important to be physically safe in the environment you find yourself in and where you want to recover and heal from traumatic experiences, healing can only occur when your environment is psychologically safe too.

In such an environment, the mind begins to heal itself, and the time and effort you invest in the healing process will bring much faster and more rewarding results.

CONFIDENCE INCREASES

Confidence expands, enabling you to address problems more effectively without feeling overwhelmed. It also combats the natural low self-esteem that is often a symptom of CPTSD. The increased confidence enables you to express yourself when you're not agreeing with what is happening to you or in your life. You reclaim the power to stand up for yourself and to clearly communicate how you want to be treated and that you won't tolerate being treated without respect.

SENSE OF BELONGING

As you enjoy a sense of belonging, sharing your emotions, fears, and every other troubling aspect of your inner landscape is easier. You'll find a valuable support network in this environment, a group you can lean on but who will also keep you accountable to maintain the necessary steps so that you empower yourself to manage your life effectively.

REDUCED STRESS

This sense of belonging that you experience in a psychologically safe environment will also automatically help to reduce your stress levels. This happens because you feel supported by the group you're part of. It is the same support that increases your resilience and helps you overcome your loneliness. You no longer have to face all the obstacles in your way alone and can call on the help of others to get you where you need to be.

KEEPS YOU FOCUSED

You'll feel more focused on the present and what you must do today to ensure a better future for yourself. When combating CPTSD on your own, it is so easy to get trapped in the memories of your traumatic experiences in your mind. These images, whether they are flashbacks or nightmares, keep you trapped and unable to progress. It is hard to focus when you're recovering from trauma unless you find yourself in a safe environment.

INCREASES SELF-WORTH

Your self-worth increases as this environment also offers the opportunity to help and support others. Helping others boosts your happiness, improves your health, and expands your sense of well-being.

Can you see how creating a safe psychological space can benefit your recovery? Each of the benefits of finding yourself in such an environment contributes to your recovery, making healing almost entirely an autonomous process, requiring far less exertion from your side.

FIVE PROVEN WAYS TO ESTABLISH MENTAL SAFETY

Since finding yourself in a mentally safe environment makes such a beneficial contribution to your journey of recovery, we must explore ways in which you can establish such a healing environment.

WAY #1: MENTAL EXERCISE

How do you picture a safe psychological space? We all have different personalities, requirements, and needs, which means that we all may have slightly different ideas of what a safe space would look like. Before you can work toward establishing such a space in your life, you need to know what it would look like to you.

Spend a couple of minutes to ponder the requirement for such a space in your life. Determine why these requirements should be met and what they mean to you. Draft a list of the necessary features and spend enough time to vividly visualize this space. Ponder what feelings you would want to enjoy from being in this space.

The more time you spend dreaming about this space and filling in the minor details of such an environment, the closer you move to realizing it in your life. Stephen Covey, author of the bestselling book, *The 7 Habits of Highly Effective People*, said, "All things are created twice. There's a mental or first creation and a physical or second creation to all things," ("Quote: 'All Things Are Created Twice,' Says Stephen R. Covey," n.d.). You're taking care of the first step to establish a space in your life by completing this step.

WAY #2: IDENTIFY FIVE PEOPLE REPRESENTING SAFETY TO YOU

This brings us back to the importance of having a support network.

- Who are the people you can count on?

- Name five people you know you could always turn to in the past or present, and they'll be there for you. What are the characteristics of these people?

- How do they contribute to your life?

- If you don't have five people to add to this list, draft a list of the values, beliefs, features, and interests of the people you naturally lean towards.

- Describe the type of relationship you would like to have with these people.

- Identify places where you can meet strangers who fit the profile.

- Also, consider how you can contribute to their lives. Friendships should be mutually beneficial, and while you can sustain the health of this relationship by contributing to the lives of others, you'll also increase your sense of self-worth.

WAY #3: NAME FIVE IDEAS TRIGGERING SAFETY

We have explored the definition of psychological safety, but you need to determine what that means to you.

- What are the things symbolic of such safety to you?

- List the thoughts, ideas, quotes, or even words you associate with safety.

- Why do these things have such deep meaning to you?

- How can you manifest these things more frequently in your life? For example, if your mind made a connection between nature and safety, what changes should you make to your routine to spend more time in nature? Identify natural spaces near you.

WAY #4: NAME THREE ACTIONS BRINING A SENSE OF SAFETY

For some people, having enough money in the bank to carry them three months into the future constitutes safety. Others may find safety in leaving a light on in their homes at night. And then some prefer to have a partner as they consider ensuring that they don't go through life as an individual as a way to bring them greater safety.

- What three top actions provide you with a sense of safety?

- What makes you feel safe when you do it?

- How can you include more of these actions in your schedule?

Remember that doing these things not only increases your sense of safety but also leaves you more empowered to take control of your life and manifest the things you desire.

WAY #5 ASK POWERFUL QUESTIONS

Sometimes safety may elude you just because of the way you see things, feel about things, or approach matters in life. Changing your perspective, a situation, event, circumstance, or person who might have robbed you of feeling safe can bring about an entirely different outcome. But before you can make this transition, you need to determine why this type of exposure makes you feel unsafe, negative, or excluded.

So, when you feel negative emotional vibrations, identify what exactly is causing you to feel this way and determine why it is the case. Some questions you can ask are:

- Why do I feel this way?
- Could I be biased at the moment?
- What other possible reasons could make them behave this way?

For example, you may feel vulnerable around your manager at work, but when you dig deeper to determine why this is the case, it may be because the person comes across as cold.

But you may feel different when you change your perspective and see that it is because they are deeply introverted. You may feel more connected to the person as you're also somewhat introverted.

These steps will help you create an environment that will optimally support your growth and healing, allowing the mind to mend after prolonged exposure to trauma.

QUICK RECAP

When exposed to an unsafe environment, it can be hard to determine what type of environment will make you feel safe. However, defining such an environment and actively working towards establishing such a space in your life is vital to your recovery.

This should be a space that isn't only physically safe and a place where you're protected but also where you can feel mentally safe, free to speak up and express yourself without fear of being shamed or reprimanded. Identifying and establishing such a space is vital for healing your mental wounds, and it is the foundation of living a happy and satisfied life with CPTSD.

12

HOW TO LIVE PEACEFULLY AND HAPPILY WITH CPTSD

The journey is never ending. There's always gonna be growth, improvement, adversity; you just gotta take it all in and do what's right, continue to grow, continue to live in the moment. –Antonio Brown

There are many reasons why people get tattoos. While some are completely against these permanent markings on their skin, others use them as a form of art to decorate their bodies or as a way to establish their identity. Then we also have a group who are addicted to the pain and those who simply consider it to be pretty.

The group I want to get to is the ones who get a tattoo symbolic to them of a certain time, event, or perhaps important life lesson. To them, their tattoo is a reminder of a life lesson learned. While a tattoo is an external reminder, sometimes the scars we carry within also serve as life lessons we've learned and grown from. While the time of injury was awful, the growth it encourages can open a new dimension of living.

JADA'S SUCCESS STORY

Jada isn't a survivor of human trafficking. She isn't a refugee and hasn't been exposed to domestic violence or sexual abuse. Nor did she live through a natural disaster. What caused Jada's CPTSD is a range of traumatic events that all bombarded her in five years.

Her mother passed away from cancer when Jada was 12. Her dad was a broken man, and in many ways, it felt to Jada that she was the one who carried him through the time of mourning. Due to his struggles to work through his sorrows, Jada's dad started drinking, which got so out of hand, he eventually lost his job. This left the two of them in a financial pickle. He couldn't find work for a couple of months, and when he did, they had to relocate to another city.

Just as she started to make friends in her new school, her dad got transferred, and they moved again. It didn't bother her as much as her dad had stopped drinking and was busy getting his life together. Jada had been attending her new school for three weeks when she got hit by a car on her way to school. She sustained serious injuries, was in a coma for three weeks, and was only discharged after two months. During this time, her dad met a woman, and it was evident they were close. Six months after Jada came home, her dad remarried. Jada and her stepmom didn't get along, but Jada didn't speak up as her dad seemed happy. A year later, her stepmom walked out on them, and Jada and her dad were alone again.

Again he started drinking, and she had to take care of the home. They repeated the exact same routine. He got fired, they didn't have any financial stability, and they relocated. By the time Jada was 18, she had lived in six different cities and had no idea what to do with her life except to care for her dad, who was still drinking but could at least hang on to the job he had. One night he didn't return home. Jada couldn't get hold of him, and it was almost midnight when the phone rang. Jada's dad was driving drunk and caused an accident, killing two innocent people. Initially, it was the shock of the events that was too much to bear, and later on, it was the shame of what her dad did that got her to pack her bags and leave.

Yet, Jada's CPTSD didn't kick in until she got a phone call three years later. Her dad had a stroke and passed away.

"I didn't know what happened to me. I wasn't sure if I felt sad, lost, or guilty for leaving my dad alone. I became edgy and couldn't sleep. I had flashbacks from memories of events long gone, and feelings surfaced that I couldn't place. I think I was repressing my emotions for the longest time, and when I got the call, my whole world came tumbling down. The worst part was that I was alone. I felt overwhelmed, scared, anxious, and exhausted. I pushed everyone away. But my employers were great, though. They insisted that I get help and offered to pay for my treatment. This changed my life. I was 21 and did not know where or what to do next. Once I was diagnosed with CPTSD, I had some direction again. It also guided my doctor to find the correct treatment for me. I went for DBT and am still taking medicine to help me to manage my condition.

It is eight years later, and I am still working at the same place, but I have been able to climb the ladder of success. The people at my company are my support network. My colleagues and the friends I've made are the ones I lean on when the day is too tough. I've learned how to identify my triggers and the feelings they stir. However, I don't hide my feelings anymore. No, I embrace them, for it is only then that they disappear entirely. My success in my career and the fact that I am engaged to get married in three months indicate that I am living a happy and fulfilled life. That and the fact that when I get up in the mornings, I'm looking forward to what the day brings. My past will always be my past. I can't escape it. But through the help I got and by keeping tabs on my emotions, life is worth living," Jada said.

The struggle with CPTSD is real and lasting, but if you employ the right tools, keep track of your emotions, and remain aware of the challenges you're facing, life can be enjoyable, fulfilling, and successful.

I've shared many strategies, tips, treatment options, and general advice to guide you toward living your best life. I know it is possible, and I want you to apply these things to set yourself free from the grip of CPTSD and empower you to control your mental health condition and manage your life effectively.

However, there are seven more strategies I want to share. By employing these strategies, you can maintain a peaceful and happy life.

SEVEN PROVEN WAYS TO LIVE A FULL LIFE WITH CPTSD

Throughout my career, I've seen many people living successful lives despite having the worst stories buried in their past. The following are the tips they've shared on how they sustain happy lives.

TIP #1: REPEAT WHAT YOU KNOW WORKS BEST

Sometimes it takes a long time to find a solution that brings the results you desire. You may have tried many things, yet nothing delivers the results you've been hoping for. And then that sweet moment arrives, and you stumble—sometimes by accident—on the best solution for you. When you do, one thing is left to do: repeat, repeat, and repeat.

The more you repeat an action, the more likely your mind will store the action, turning it into an auto-response, and gradually the amount of effort this action takes to complete becomes less as you're so familiar with the steps necessary to bring you the results you desire.

When managing your CPTSD, there will be days when it goes so well you may believe you've beaten CPTSD and freed yourself from the inner scars. But the thing about scars is that they are permanent, causing you to stumble again. That is okay. It indicates you must return to basics and repeat what works for you.

TIP #2: CHALLENGE YOUR SENSE OF HELPLESSNESS

As much as you were a victim of past events, exposed to trauma, and trapped in a situation you couldn't escape, you're now free from these constraints. So, even if you still feel helpless, it is likely not true. But you need to realize this to empower yourself.

The only way to realize your freedom is to challenge your helplessness. Coupled with your extensive knowledge of coping strategies and the many tools you've added to your mental health toolbox, you're perfectly empowered to claim control of your life. Sure, there will be times when you feel tired or overwhelmed, but these are merely indicators that you're active on the playing field.

This reminds me of the famous speech by Teddy Roosevelt, "The credit belongs to the man who is actually in the arena, whose face is marred by dust and sweat and blood; who strives valiantly; who errs, who comes short again and again," ("The Man in the Arena Meaning | Theodore Roosevelt Quotes," n.d.).

Being in the arena takes its toll, but what you see in the mirror isn't helplessness, it is exhaustion, and all you need is a little rest.

TIP #3: CONNECT WITH OTHERS LIKE YOU

You're not a lonely traveler on a desolate road. No, life is brutal, leaving many with similar injuries to yours. Find these people. Seek them in support groups, online networks, or the cubicle beside yours. The journey with CPTSD is long, but it doesn't have to be alone.

TIP #4: GO FOR THERAPY

Therapy organizes the mind, cleanses it of impurity, helps it understand what happened, restructures it, and gives it confidence. It's a weapon you need to use!

If you're unsure whether therapy is necessary, draft a list comparing the pros and cons. What do you stand to lose? But what you can gain is immense. Therapy can be your lifeline when matters slip beyond your control, where you can recharge and find your footing again when you slip. There is no shame in seeing someone. You're not seeing a therapist because you're broken or damaged. Still, because you have the wisdom and understanding that you're capable of far more and with the help of a professional, you're exploring the possibilities.

TIP #5: SET GOALS TO KEEP YOU DIRECTED

Someone without a goal always reminds me of an object floating in the ocean. There is no direction or purpose. It is controlled by the current and goes where the waves take it. It can track its progress, for there is no intention behind its movement. So, there remains a constant lack of accomplishment.

But your compass is set in a certain direction when you have a goal. You have clarity of where you're heading, and this guides what you should do to get there. Often, you can look back and see how far you've come; this sense of achievement drives you to even bigger goals.

TIP #6: BE YOUR OWN BEST FRIEND

Be your own best friend. Understand yourself. Know yourself. Spend time with yourself! Be kind to yourself. Direct your thoughts to be encouraging, caring, and considerate when you talk to yourself. Use positive affirmation to uplift your inner narrative.

Always try to get in touch with your inner self! Journalling is a wonderful tool to achieve this. Do not run into any kind of addiction! Constantly embrace your pain, but do the same with your joy too.

TIP #7: NEVER GIVE UP!

Did you have a bad day? Make sure you learn from it and look to what's next. Are you tired of so many inner efforts? Get some rest. Don't give up on everything you've worked for. Come back. Put your shoes on and get back to recovery as fast as possible.

Never confuse the need to take a break with the need to quit trying; instead, work toward achieving the desired outcome—a fulfilling, joyous, and rewarding life!

QUICK RECAP

It can be easy to lose hope when comparing your life with someone else's. It may appear that their lives are running so smoothly, everything just falls into place for them. How do you ever compete with that, right?

You don't. Never compete with anyone else except the person you were yesterday. Not because you're bound to fail when you measure up against another, but because you don't know what is happening behind closed doors.

It may appear as if someone has a perfect life, but it is merely a facade covering up the hurtful details of reality. Therefore, don't waste your time and energy on an unfair challenge; challenge yourself every day. Take breaks to rest, but come back and continue the journey, for life is for the living, and you have all to gain by staking your claim of joy, happiness, love, success, and power in your life.

CONCLUSION

How long were you trapped in trauma? Was it days, weeks, months, or years?

You can never make up for the lost time. But you weren't in control of your life back then. It wasn't your choice. But now you're free to determine your destiny.

Never underestimate the impact these events had on your life. But keep in mind how many years you still have ahead of you. When you lose a button, you don't throw away the shirt, right? When your truck gets stuck in the mud, you don't chuck the truck, right? Why would you want to throw away so many good years because of what happened in the past?

You've lost a mentionable amount of time already. There is no need to lose anymore.

This book serves as a guide to help you understand what you're going through, why you're going through it, and how it impacts your mental and physical health. What is way more important, though, is that it also covers the many steps you can take to improve your situation. These steps serve as handy tools to maintain mental and physical health, remain in control of your life, and help you live life with fulfillment.

These are the tools:

- Understanding CPTSD and its symptoms is vital to know where you're at in life. By doing this, you gain familiarity with your departure point on this journey.

- You learned how the nervous system works and how you can create new neural pathways, to change your habits, behavior, and perspectives.

- Trauma and how it impacts your body are now familiar concepts to you too. This knowledge helps you employ greater awareness of any symptoms that surface at times.

- The mind-body connection is an essential tool to improve your mental health by using your body. Now you know how to utilize this effectively.

- We've covered the necessary steps to establish an emotional support network and looked at how this can benefit you.

- No healing will occur until you consciously choose to get better.

- A combination of therapy and medication will form the backbone of your treatment. One type of therapy to consider is emotional exposure therapy. In the chapter on this therapy, you've explored the benefits of facing your fears.

- Emotions denied tend to flare up in an exaggerated form when least expected. It is vital to communicate your inner world to those around you. It also helps them to better understand how they can support you effectively.

- Experiencing negative emotions is part of life. Embrace yours, but don't forget to celebrate your positive emotions too.

- Seek a safe psychological space. Or, maybe you need to create such a space for yourself. It is how you can speed up healing and sustain a balanced life.

Living with CPTSD adds an additional responsibility to life. It demands that you utilize the tools you have consistently, maintain a sense of awareness of your emotions, and take timeouts when necessary. That said, living with CPTSD can be a very successful venture, one you can enjoy like many others just like you.

So, what are you waiting for? Choose to heal, set your intentions on recovery, and take the steps this journey requires.

REFERENCES

Abraham, M. (2020, October 10). *How to perform exposure therapy for anxiety at home.* Calm Clinic. https://www.calmclinic.com/anxiety/treatment/exposure-therapy

Adverse childhood experiences (ACEs). (2021, August 23). Centers for Disease Control and Prevention. https://www.cdc.gov/vitalsigns/aces/index.html

Alangui, M. (2021, October 29). *Top 10 reasons why change is difficult.* LinkedIn. https://www.linkedin.com/pulse/top-10-reasons-why-change-difficult-mari-alangui/

All About Psychology. (n.d.). *Pin on Learning and Development.* Pinterest. https://www.pinterest.es/pin/17521886039917290/

American Psychiatric Association. (2022, November). *What is posttraumatic stress disorder (PTSD)?* https://www.psychiatry.org/patients-families/ptsd/what-is-ptsd

American Psychological Association. (2017, July). *What is cognitive behavioral therapy?* https://www.apa.org/ptsd-guideline/patients-and-families/cognitive-behavioral

Avendano, K. (2023, March 21). *45 Inspirational mental health quotes that are supportive and empowering.* Good Housekeeping. https://www.goodhousekeeping.com/life/a39739060/mental-health-quotes/

Cleveland Clinic Medical Professional. (2022, September 3). *EMDR therapy: What it is, procedure & effectiveness.* Cleveland Clinic. https://my.clevelandclinic.org/health/treatments/22641-emdr-therapy

Cleveland Clinic Medical Professional. (2023a, May 4). *Complex PTSD.* Cleveland Clinic.

https://my.clevelandclinic.org/health/diseases/24881-cptsd-complex-ptsd

Cleveland Clinic Medical Professional. (2023b, May 4). *CPTSD (Complex PTSD)*. Cleveland Clinic. https://my.clevelandclinic.org/health/diseases/24881-cptsd-complex-ptsd

CPTSD Vs BPD: Top 5 things you need to know. (2022, February 21). Makin Wellness. https://www.makinwellness.com/cptsd-vs-bpd/

Davis, S. (2020, December 28). *The Neurotransmitters of seasonal affective disorder and complex post-traumatic stress disorder*. CPTSD Foundation. https://cptsdfoundation.org/2020/12/28/the-neurotransmitters-of-seasonal-affective-disorder-and-complex-post-traumatic-stress-disorder/

Embogama. (2016, August 5). *Difference between conscious and subconscious mind*. Pediaa. https://pediaa.com/difference-between-conscious-and-subconscious-mind/

EMDR Institute. (2019). *What is EMDR?* https://www.emdr.com/what-is-emdr/

Flâneur Life Team. (2022, June 21). *61 Killer quotes about overcoming fear*. Flaneur Life.

https://www.flaneurlife.com/overcoming-fear-quotes/

Gallo, A. (2023, February 15). *What is psychological safety?* Harvard Business Review. https://hbr.org/2023/02/what-is-psychological-safety

Gillette, H. (2021, September 10). *Symptoms of complex post-traumatic stress disorder.* Psych Central. https://psychcentral.com/ptsd/complex-posttraumatic-stress-disorder-symptoms#common-triggers

Hilton Andersen, C. (2023, February 24). *20 Relationship communication quotes to strengthen your love.* The Healthy. https://www.thehealthy.com/family/relationships/relationship-communication-quotes/

Hinojosa, R. (2018). Cardiovascular disease among United States military veterans: Evidence of a waning healthy soldier effect using the National Health Interview Survey. *Chronic Illness, 16*(1), 55–68. https://doi.org/10.1177/1742395318785237

How to explain trauma to a partner. (2022, September 14). Mind Well NYC. https://mindwellnyc.com/how-to-explain-trauma-to-a-partner/

Jim Carrey Quote: "It's our intention. Our intention is everything. Nothing happens on this planet without it. Not one single thing has eve..." (n.d.). Quote Fancy. https://quotefancy.com/quote/1123572/Jim-Carrey-It-s-our-intention-Our-intention-is-everything-Nothing-happens-on-this-planet

Keohan, E. (2022, September 14). *How to deal with trauma: 5 Coping tips.* Talkspace. https://www.talkspace.com/blog/how-to-deal-with-trauma/

Lane, C. (2020, November 30). *PTSD contributes to suicide risk, particularly for women.* UCL News. https://www.ucl.ac.uk/news/2020/nov/ptsd-contributes-suicide-risk-particularly-women

Lawhorn, D. S. (n.d.). *Massaging emotions to the surface.* Massage Chair Store. https://massagechairstore.com/massaging-emotions-to-the-surface/

Lebow, H. I. (2021a, May 27). *What is complex trauma and how does it develop.* Psych Central. https://psychcentral.com/ptsd/complex-trauma-a-step-by-step-description-of-how-it-develops#how-does-it-develop

Lebow, H. I. (2021b, June 2). *What is complex trauma and how does it develop.* Psych Central. https://psychcentral.com/ptsd/complex-trauma-a-step-by-step-description-of-how-it-develops#how-does-it-develop

Leonard, J. (2022, December 23). *What is complex PTSD: Symptoms, treatment, and resources to help you cope.* Medical News Today. https://www.medicalnewstoday.com/articles/322886

Man In the Arena meaning | Theodore Roosevelt Quotes. (n.d.). Ageless Investing. https://agelessinvesting.com/the-man-in-the-arena/

Marsolek, A. (2022, July 20). *Can massage relieve symptoms of depression, anxiety and stress?* Mayo Clinic Health System. https://www.mayoclinichealthsystem.org/hometown-health/speaking-of-health/massage-for-depression-anxiety-and-stress

Marter, J. (2021, November 23). *7 Ways to ask for emotional support.* Psychology Today. https://www.psychologytoday.com/za/blog/mental-wealth/202111/7-ways-ask-emotional-support

Mental Health Match. (2022, June 13). *101 Inspiring mental health quotes.* https://mentalhealthmatch.com/articles/anxiety/inspiring-mental-health-quotes

Mind body spirit quotes. (n.d.). A-Z Quotes. https://www.azquotes.com/quotes/topics/mind-body-spirit.html

MyLife Psychologists. (n.d.). *What are the benefits of dialectical behaviour therapy (DBT)?* https://mylifepsychologists.com.au/what-are-the-benefits-of-dialectical-behaviour-therapy-dbt/

Novotney, A. (n.d.). *The risks of social isolation.* American Psychological Association. https://www.apa.org/monitor/2019/05/ce-corner-isolation

Nunez, K. (2020, August 10). *The benefits of progressive muscle relaxation and how to do it.* Healthline. https://www.healthline.com/health/progressive-muscle-relaxation#about-pmr

Parincu, Z. (n.d.). *Emotional support: Definition, examples, and theories.* The Berkeley Well-Being Institute. https://www.berkeleywellbeing.com/emotional-support.html

Pisano, T. (n.d.). *Why you shouldn't suppress your emotions.* M1 Psychology. https://m1psychology.com/why-you-shouldnt-suppress-your-emotions/

Post-traumatic Stress Disorder (PTSD). (2022, December 13). Mayo Clinic. https://www.mayoclinic.org/diseases-conditions/post-traumatic-stress-disorder/symptoms-causes/syc-20355967

Quote: "All things are created twice," says Stephen R. Covey. (n.d.). Studio 2D. https://studio2d.com/quote-all-things-are-created-twice-says-stephen-r-covey/

Safe places quotes. (n.d.). A-Z Quotes. https://www.azquotes.com/quotes/topics/safe-places.html

Serenity prayer – Applying 3 truths from the Bible. (2022, October 22). Crosswalk.com. https://www.crosswalk.com/faith/prayer/serenity-prayer-applying-3-truths-from-the-bible.html

Sharpe, R. (2021, February 27). *100+ PTSD quotes to help you cope with trauma.* Declutter the Mind. https://declutterthemind.com/blog/ptsd-quotes/

Smith, M., Robbins, L., & Segal, J. (2023, February 24). *How to cope with traumatic events.* Help Guide. https://www.helpguide.org/articles/ptsd-trauma/traumatic-stress.htm

Symptoms, signs & effects of psychological trauma. (n.d.). Cascade Behavioral Health Hospital. https://www.cascadebh.com/behavioral/trauma/signs-symptoms-effects/

Tanasugarn, A. (2021, September 25). *The reasons people with complex PTSD self-isolate.* Invisible Illness. https://medium.com/invisible-illness/the-reasons-people-with-complex-ptsd-self-isolate-846266b52a6d

10 Questions to ask when choosing a therapist. (2022, December 7). Harvard Health. https://www.health.harvard.edu/mind-and-mood/10-questions-to-ask-when-choosing-a-therapist

THC Editorial Team. (2022, February 2). *Polyvagal theory exercises: Benefits and examples.* The Human Condition. https://thehumancondition.com/polyvagal-theory-exercises-benefits-examples/

Tull, M. (2023, February 15). *What is complex PTSD (C-PTSD)?* Verywell Mind. https://www.verywellmind.com/what-is-complex-ptsd-2797491

WebMD Editorial Contributors. (2023, May 12). *What to know about complex PTSD and its symptoms.* WebMD. https://www.webmd.com/mental-health/what-to-know-complex-ptsd-symptoms

Wong, P. (n.d.). *What happens if you embrace and accept your negative emotions?* Pinterest. https://www.pinterest.ca/pin/173881235596980369/

Printed in Great Britain
by Amazon